ARL ANIMAL RESCU

D1504633

For Love of
CATS

Landauer Publishing, LLC

ARL ANIMAL RESCUE LEAGUE OF IOWA, INC.™

For Love of
CATS

This book was designed, produced,
and published by Landauer Publishing, LLC
3100 101st Street, Urbandale, IA 50322
www.landauercorp.com   515/287/2144   800/557/2144

President/Publisher: Jeramy Lanigan Landauer
Vice President of Sales and Administration: Kitty Jacobson
Editor: Jeri Simon
Contributing Editor: Carol McGarvey
Art Director: Laurel Albright
Photographer: Sue Voegtlin

ISBN 13: 978-1-935726-13-5
ISBN 10:   1-935726-13-7

Library of Congress Control Number: 2011937122
This book printed on acid-free paper.
Printed in China

10-9-8-7-6-5-4-3-2-1

Table of Contents

Table of Contents

Table of Contents

Table of Contents

Table of Contents

ANIMAL RESCUE LEAGUE OF IOWA, INC.™

Founded in 1926, The Animal Rescue League of Iowa, Inc. (ARL) is Iowa's largest nonprofit animal shelter.

The ARL serves animals in need across the state, with a focus on Polk County and central Iowa. The mission of the ARL is to promote animal welfare, encourage and strengthen the human/animal bond and prevent the overpopulation of pets.

Last year, the ARL took in over 20,000 animals from 61 Iowa counties and 9 states. Of the 20,000 animals, 9,709 were cats and kittens. On any given day, the shelter has more than 650 animals in its care at its main facility and four satellite locations. With such a large number of animals to care for and only 50 full-time staff members for five locations, the ARL relies heavily on volunteers to assist in all realms of the organization, from daily care of animals to helping with fundraising efforts. Currently, more than 1,700 volunteers donate thousands of hours of service.

The ARL is the only shelter in central Iowa that never turns away an animal in need. This results in a large number of animals and people who depend on the ARL each year. This dependence has grown dramatically since the ARL was founded more than 80 years ago.

—Tom Colvin, Executive Director
Animal Rescue League of Iowa

ARL-Iowa never turns away an animal in need.

The saying on the front desk, "Finding Your Best Friend • Share Your Love • Be A Friend", welcomes visitors.

Yvette guides families through the animal adoption process.

Indoor exercise and training center

In the Hug Room, adopters and animals meet and interact.

This beautiful Siamese mix cat is in an adoption kennel waiting for her forever family.

Caternity

Litters of kittens are kept together and socialized by volunteers until adopted.

Betty is one of ARL's resident cats. She is a regular on the ARL's Facebook page and has become quite famous.

ARL-Iowa's agility course inside Bailey's Bark Park.

The ARL-Iowa Rescue Ranch cares for abused and neglected horses taken from their owners by the court system until they are ready for adoption.

Spacious outdoor dog runs provide daily exercise areas.

The ARL-Animal House Retail Store offers specially selected equipment, supplies, toys and treats.

Photo by: Kelly Kesling,
Kesling Photography

Tom Colvin

Tom Colvin has been instrumental in the State of Iowa for animal protection work for more than 40 years. He began his work on animal protection as a veterinary technician in Waterloo, Iowa. He went on to become the director of the Black Hawk Humane Society (now called Cedar Bend). Tom moved to Des Moines in January, 1993, to become the shelter director of the Animal Rescue League of Iowa, Inc. (ARL). In 1995, he was appointed the ARL's executive director, a position he still holds. Tom led the initiative to build a new 43,000-square-foot shelter, which was completed in October, 2008.

The Animal Rescue League is the largest animal shelter in the State of Iowa with four adoption locations and is responsible for the care of more than 20,000 animals each year, including a farm animal adoption program, and animal control for the City of Des Moines. Additionally, Tom started a prison program at Rockwell City Men's Prison, called Whinny, which provides extra care and rehabilitation for neglected horses that come to the ARL until they are ready for adoption.

Tom has been the President of the Iowa Federation of Humane Societies since 1981, is on the Iowa State University External Stakeholders Advisory Group and the Board of the Iowa Wildlife Center. He has also served on the Iowa Board of Veterinary Medicine. In addition, Tom was a wildlife rehabilitator and has served on Iowa deer task force committees. Tom has done extensive work on animal cruelty investigations and puppy mills.

He has worked tirelessly on legislation to strengthen Iowa's laws for animal protection. He has received awards for his efforts in legislation, including his work to enact the animal shelter mandatory spay/neuter law in 1992 and the felony animal abuse law in 2000. Recent successes in legislation have resulted in prohibiting giving pets as prizes, felony animal fighting laws, and in 2010, the passing of the Puppy Mill Bill.

Photo by: Kelly Kesling,
Kesling Photography

Carol Griglione

Carol Griglione has worked on a wide range of animal issues in Iowa over the past 20 years, including those affecting animal shelters. She has been involved in such areas as making animal torture and dog fighting a felony in Iowa.

For the past 15 years, she has specifically focused on cats. She is president of the board of directors of the Animal Rescue League of Iowa, Inc., is on the board of the Iowa Federation of Humane Societies and regularly speaks on cat behavior on local radio stations.

Carol holds a bachelors degree in communications from Simpson College in Indianola, Iowa, and a masters in non-profit management from Drake University in Des Moines.

Carol started volunteering with the Animal Rescue League of Iowa 20 years ago. She threw herself into study at the ARL, attending conferences and seminars around the United States, learning from other behavior experts and from reading.

Carol coordinates the ARL's Catsnip Spay/Neuter Program and Summer Cat Getaway Program.

Carol credits her first cat, Azzurro, with her passion for understanding cats and their behavior and helping people learn about them to keep them in their homes and out of shelters.

A native Iowan, Carol resides in Runnells with her husband and their three dogs, seven cats, three horses and twelve pet chickens.

Photo by: Kelly Kesling, Kesling Photography

Mick McAuliffe

Mick McAuliffe joined the ARL staff in November, 2009, as the Pet Behavior and Enrichment Manager. Before coming to the United States, Mick served as the Director of Animal Behavior and Training for the R.S.P.C.A. Queensland, Australia, where he developed assessment, modification and training programs for multiple species. In addition to his extensive work in canine training, Mick has applied his training skills to a variety of animals, from Sea World Australia's large marine mammals to serving as head avian keeper and trainer for a collection of 130 native and exotic birds and developing free-flight shows for visitors.

Mick has lectured on animal behavior across five continents, working extensively in Australia, Japan, China, England, Saudi Arabia, and the United States. He believes pets live with us as part of our family, learning what we like and dislike through everyday experiences. He does not believe in dictatorships or set training sessions. Instead, he educates owners on how to teach pets our rules and guidelines each day. Whether you are sitting on your sofa or going for a walk, living is learning.

In Afghanistan, his experiences handling and training bomb-detecting dogs changed him forever. He says, "I wouldn't be here right now if it weren't for a couple of the dogs I worked with."

Training should be fun for you and your pet, not stressful. Mick teaches using only positive reinforcement techniques, eliminating the need for physical or verbal correction or training equipment that can cause pain or injury. He educates owners on how to teach their pets with patience and understanding, resulting in a well-mannered pet and a life-long bond.

Mick and his wife Caitlin share their home with four cats, their dog Lucy, and their birds Jack and Zane. All are rescues.

ARL

ANIMAL RESCUE LEAGUE OF IOWA, INC.

Some of the Current ARL Programs and Services

- Pet Adoptions at four Des Moines-area locations.

- Pet Behavior Counseling and Training classes (for dogs, cats and rabbits).

- Spay and Neuter Programs include Catsnip, PitStop, The Purr Project, The Daily Fix and Spay the Mother.

- Humane Education.

- Lost & Found and ID Me Program.

- Pet Receiving (of strays and owner-released animals).

- Pet First Aid Training.

- Cruelty Intervention Program.

- Disaster Planning Service for Pets.

- Whinny Program in collaboration with Iowa prison system.

- Volunteer Opportunities.

- Pets in Crisis (provide temporary housing for pets of people in crisis, i.e. house fire, domestic abuse, homelessness).

- Temporary Love and Care Program for special needs animals.

- Animal Assisted Therapy.

- Humane Euthanasia and Cremation Service.

- Legislation/Advocacy for animal welfare laws.

- Contractual relationship with several local governmental entities including the City of Des Moines to provide care and all Animal Control services to over 7,500 lost and homeless animals. These animals are found by the public or picked up or seized by the Animal Rescue League of Iowa Animal Control Officers, who provide the service for Des Moines.

- Horse Rescue and Adoption Program.

- Barn Buddy Program.

Some of the Current ARL Clubs and Services

Many times black cats seem to be overlooked in favor of lighter colored cats. There are different theories behind this, maybe it's because their facial expressions are harder to see, so there isn't an instant connection. No matter what the theory, the fact remains, black cats are the most commonly overlooked cats in shelters. Cats come in all sorts of sizes and colors and each has its own unique personality. It is this personality that draws us to them, not the color of their fur. Remember this the next time you are looking to add a new family member. Take a good look at who is in that kennel. You might just find your new best friend.

Have you ever been to the shelter, walked down a line of kennels and seen mostly black dogs? Many times black dogs seem to be overlooked in favor of lighter colored dogs. There are different theories behind this, maybe it's because they are harder to see in the back of their kennel, so there isn't an instant connection. It is a dog's unique personality that draws us to him, not the color of his fur. Remember this the next time you are looking to adopt a new family member. Don't overlook the dog that could become your new best friend.

Pit bull terriers are perhaps the most misunderstood dog breed in the world. With proper training and responsible ownership, these dogs can be lifelong companions to people of all ages. The Animal Rescue League believes that a breed alone does not make a dog good or bad. It is our hope that through education, compassion and understanding, pit bull terriers will soon be respected for the amazing animals they truly are. Some have given them a bad reputation, now it is up to you to fix it.

CatSnip is a no-cost spay/neuter program provided by The Animal Rescue League of Iowa and sponsored by Petsmart Charities. It is provided for any persons who are participants in any financial assistance program and living in certain zip code areas. Any donations received are put back into the CatSnip program to provide continued funding for this much needed service.

The purpose of the Summer Cat Getaway program is to give long-term ARL cats still waiting for a home a chance to get out of the shelter during the ARL's busiest time of year and enjoy the in-home life they deserve. Approximately 50 new cats arrive each day in the summer and the Summer Getaway program allows the ARL to bring more cats in for adoption.

In 2010, the ARL opened a dog park called "Bailey's Bark Park", named after an ARL Alumni, Bailey. Bailey's Bark Park is primarily a place for dogs in adoption to be able to get out and run and play without the restrictions of a leash.

LOYAL FRIENDS CLUB

Make a lasting impact on the animals by becoming a part of the ARL's Loyal Friends Club! You can join the club by simply making a reoccurring, monthly donation of your choice to the Animal Rescue League of Iowa.

For Shelter Cats Everywhere

This book is dedicated to all shelter cats—the ones who are waiting for a good home and the ones who have already found one. To all the once homeless animals, don't give up on humans. Your unconditional love inspires us to strive to do more, not only for you, but for every animal that will follow behind you.

A Hands-On Journey

For years cats have been portrayed as standoffish, aloof or even "bad luck". For those of us that have loved and worked with cats for most of our lives, we know these portrayals are unfair to felines.

We are writing this book for the purpose of helping those that love cats and those we hope will learn to adore them for the wonderful loving, curious, playful and sensitive creatures they are.

Neither Mick nor Carol is a veterinarian. But what they offer that most others cannot is guidance and advice built upon more than 40 years cumulatively of working hands-on with these animals in many environments. This book contains the knowledge they have learned in their journey of working with cats. They want to share this knowledge with others to better the lives of both humans and cats.

"A national leader"

"The Humane Society of the United States has partnered with the Animal Rescue League of Iowa, Inc. (ARL) for more than a decade on companion animal welfare initiatives. The ARL has proven itself a national leader in the animal sheltering field with innovative programs on pet adoption, shelter enrichment for animals, companion animal legislation, spay/neuter outreach and other initiatives that will better the lives of animals today and in the future. We are pleased to see the ARL publish a book that will help keep cats and dogs in their current homes while providing the enrichment they need to thrive."

Michael Markarian,
executive vice-president and
chief operating officer of
The Humane Society of the United States

"A state of the art facility"

"I was pleasantly surprised to find one of the best animal shelters I have ever encountered in an area considered to be the hinterlands by those of us who frequent the Washington-New York City corridor. The Animal Rescue League in Des Moines, Iowa, goes beyond being a state-of-the-art facility that pays special attention to the behavioral needs of the animals in its care. The cats in particular were happy, healthy, relaxed and had plenty of opportunities for interaction. The staff as well was tuned in to what it takes to help the creatures in their care find life-long loving homes."

Randall Lockwood, Ph.D., CAAB
Senior Vice President/Forensic Sciences and
Anti-Cruelty Projects
American Society for
Prevention of Cruelty to Animals

Some happy endings
from the Animal Rescue League of Iowa

Alley

Polk County Animal Control received a call from Waste Connections saying they had found a bag of kittens someone had carelessly put out with their trash. There were six kittens total, but sadly only one was alive. The men at Waste Connections quickly rescued the kitten, gave her a bath, and called Polk County Animal Control to pick her up. The kitten, now named "Alley", was brought to ARL, was cared for in a foster home until she could be nursed back to health and was then placed up for adoption where she found her loving home.

Ash

Ash was found September 2010 by a Good Samaritan who saw her struggling to crawl out of a burning bush pile. He rushed her to the Animal Rescue League so she could have a chance at survival. The kitten, estimated to be only 3 weeks old, had burned ears, paws, and tail but was otherwise doing remarkably well. The medical staff treated her wounds and placed her in a staff person's home for round the clock care until she recovered from her wounds and was old enough to eat on her own. Her foster mom bottle-fed her every day while her German Shepherd gave her comfort, warmth, and love—the dog even licked Ash's wounds to clean them each day. A true demonstration of compassion from a giant dog towards a tiny, injured kitten.

Eight weeks later, Ash was still in her foster home as she neared the end of her recovery. Parts of her tail and ears had fallen off due to the burn damage, but she was otherwise a happy, health kitty who loved cats and both big and small dogs! She was soon placed in adoption where she found a family of her own and a bed to lay in.

choosing the right cat or kitten for you

An Easy Decision?

It seems like a simple decision really.

You decide you want a feline friend to add to your family. You go to the shelter, find one you like, and you are done. Only it is not that simple, and quite honestly, it should not be that easy. The cat you choose will be a member of your family for an average of fifteen years. If you decide to add a feline to your family, do it with the intention that it is for the lifetime of the cat, no exceptions.

Cats end up in shelters for a variety of reasons, the most common being litter box or behavior issues. With just a little effort and re-training on the part of the owner, many of these issues can be solved. If there are behavior issues, be committed to solving them.

Age and personality are two important things to consider when adding another cat to your family.

Consider your lifestyle when choosing a pet. Mature cats adapt more quickly to their family's busy lifestyles.

What to Consider
When Choosing a Cat

Your lifestyle. Are you home a lot, or are you gone much of the time with work and other activities? Do you have other pets? Do you have children at home or plan on having children in the future?

Many people want to adopt a kitten, because they believe the kitten will bond with them more so than an adult cat. That is just not true. Adult cats absolutely bond with their new family, just as a kitten would.

People often choose kittens because they are cute. But, as we all know, kittens grow up to be cats. And if you find your lifestyle is such that you are not home a lot, a kitten will become lonely and bored. This is when behavior issues start to surface. For people that are away from home with busy lifestyles, a mature cat is the way to go.

With kittens, we encourage people to adopt two at the same time. They will bond with the humans in their lives, as well as with each other. They will keep each other company when you are away from the house for long hours. At night, when you are trying to sleep, they will play with each other.

Children. Children are a big consideration in choosing a pet. Consider the ages of your children and their level of play.

If your child is five-years-old and likes to wrestle and play hard, a six-week-old kitten probably is not the right pet. A cat that has already been around children is always a good choice.

Often at shelters, we hear, "I told my child she could get a pet, but she will have to take care of him." That is an unrealistic expectation and often results in the pet being returned days, weeks, or months later. It is hard for pets to go in and out of a home. They bond with their humans and when they find themselves at a shelter, they become stressed at being taken away from home and the people they love. When an 'easy-way-out' decision is made to give up a pet, we are teaching our children that animals can be given away, turned away, and gotten rid of at the drop of a hat. If you are considering getting a cat or kitten, go into it fully aware that the adults in the home will have to help with the care of the pet.

Cats that have already been around children are always a good adoption choice.

What to Consider When Choosing a Cat Continued

Other pets. You must also consider the other pets in your household when choosing an additional pet. If you have a breed of dog that is aggressive by nature to cats, it is important you choose a cat that has been around dogs in the past. Some people question whether they should even get a cat with a dog already in the home. Cats and dogs can be friends. In fact, they can be great friends. The belief that they are natural enemies has been portrayed in movies for years, but it just isn't true. Cats and dogs will form relationships, even sleeping together, grooming each other, and taking care of each other.

We have seen this happen at the ARL. Opie, an American Eskimo, and Elmo, a cat, were brought to the ARL by the same family. When they arrived, the staff took Opie to the dog kennels and Elmo to the cat cages for evaluation. Over the next few days, both were depressed and refused to eat. Opie got to the point where he wouldn't even raise his head when the staff came to feed him. The director suggested taking Elmo to the dog kennels and putting him in with Opie. Instantly, both were happy pets. They slept together, ate together, and all was good as long as they were together. The ARL adopted out this dog and cat as "bonded buddies" to a new home.

Such events like these are not uncommon, and they certainly show the bond animals can form in taking care of each other.

For those of you who are still skeptical about the bonds between animals, let me share a couple stories involving my own pets.

Spirit was a Greyhound/Collie mix, and Zorra, a tortoiseshell cat, lived in the same household. One day Zorra was trying to jump on the coffee table. She was a little uncoordinated, so she didn't always complete her jumps. After three attempts, Spirit, lying nearby, got up and lifted Zorra onto the table with her nose.

Another example of a friendship between a dog and a cat was evident when Azzurro, normally an inside cat, escaped outside one night when his dog friends were let out. The dogs were called in and immediately started bothering us, whining, going to the door, and circling around. We couldn't figure out why, but decided to go to the door to see what was up. When we opened the door, the dogs ran outside, straight to where Azzurro was, and began nosing him back to the door to come inside.

Altering is a Must

Whether you adopt a cat or kitten, spaying and neutering is a must.

Spaying and neutering help control the overpopulation of cats in this country. It can also help with some behavior problems.

— CAT FACTS —

There are approximately 86 million owned cats in the U.S.

Consider the Mix

Amy found a kitten and fell in love.

She took the kitten home, named him Hershey, and planned on keeping him. The problem was Amy already had three Whippets. The Whippets were certain this new kitten was a toy for them. Being sight hounds, Whippets love to chase and often cause harm to small furry things that run away from them.

For two years, Amy had to keep these pets separated. She gradually introduced them to each other, tethering the dogs to her so they couldn't chase Hershey and cause harm. Gradually, this process worked and now everyone lives in harmony. The Whippets have learned that Hershey is part of the family. This is an extreme example of what you need to consider with pets already at home. Are you willing to tether dogs to you and keep watch closely for however long it takes?

Contrary to what is portrayed in the movies, cats and dogs can develop a bond and become great friends.

Mewsings
Add Another Cat?

Age and Personality Matter

Question: Betty called in to the Companion Connection radio program one Saturday after hearing us discuss the benefits of adding another cat to a one cat family. Betty wasn't home much due to her work schedule and her cat Boscoe was home alone a lot. Boscoe was a neutered, five-year-old male, and was still playful. Betty was looking for suggestions on finding a good match for Boscoe. She was wondering if she should get a female, as she had heard that two males in the house might be stressful. She was also hoping to get another kitten.

Answer: Betty should consider getting an adult cat between the ages of two and seven, with gender not being an issue. For cats, it isn't about the gender, it is more about the age and personality. Does your current cat want to play all the time, sometimes, or never? Try to match your resident cat's personality to the cat you are considering adding to your family. Get a second cat that wants to play the same general amount of time as the one you already have. Matching personalities will enable the cats to make an easier connection.

What to Consider When Choosing a Cat Continued

Age of the Cat. Consider the age of the cat you want to adopt and the ages of the other members of your pet family. People sometimes prepare for the loss of a senior cat by adopting a kitten. The last thing an older cat wants is a six-week-old kitten that pesters and bugs him. While the gender of a cat you are adopting isn't an issue, age certainly is. Look at the age and personality of your current cat, and get a playmate that will complement him.

Adopting a cat similar in age and temperament to your current cat will make the bonding process easier.

Breeds of Cats

Many purebred cats find themselves in animal shelters. Be sure to check out the cats at the animal shelter before looking elsewhere.

While animal shelters do get purebred cats on a regular basis, consider adopting a mixed breed cat. Cats, whatever their breed, are fun and curious creatures, and can form a bond with the humans in their lives. Whatever type of cat you choose, a cat you adopt from a shelter is sure to give you many years of joy.

ABYSSINIAN
shorthair; busy, active,
and affectionate.

AMERICAN BOBTAIL
longhair and shorthair;
loving and intelligent.

AMERICAN CURL
longhair and shorthair;
affectionate, and energetic.

AMERICAN SHORTHAIR
shorthair; relatively quiet and
even-tempered in nature.

AMERICAN WIREHAIR
shorthair; with an
even temperament.

BALINESE
longhair; vocal, active,
and affectionate.

BIRMAN
longhair; sweet
and affectionate.

BOMBAY
shorthair; playful, affectionate,
and likes to sit on laps.

BRITISH SHORTHAIR
shorthair; calm, quiet,
and enjoys humans.

BURMESE
shorthair; people-oriented
and affectionate.

CHARTREUX
shorthair; bonds with
humans quickly.

COLORPOINT SHORTHAIR
shorthair; vocal, affectionate,
active, and persistent.

CORNISH REX
shorthair; active
and affectionate.

DEVON REX
shorthair; full of personality.

EGYPTIAN MAU
shorthair; active,
athletic, likes to play.

EUROPEAN BURMESE
shorthair; highly intelligent,
affectionate, and loyal.

EXOTIC
shorthair; quiet in nature, sweet,
and affectionate.

HAVANA BROWN
shorthair; busy, affectionate,
and loves their humans.

JAPANESE BOBTAIL
longhair and shorthair; active,
intelligent, and affectionate.

JAVANESE
longhair; vocal,
active, persistent, and loving.

KORAT
shorthair; energetic,
playful, and affectionate.

LA PERM
longhair and shorthair; lap cats,
playful, active, and gentle.

MAINE COON
longhair, gentle and
easy going but full of
personality and active.

MANX
longhair and shorthair;
quiet and gentle.

choosing the right cat or kitten for you

NORWEGIAN FOREST CAT
longhair; active and sweet.

OCICAT
shorthair; strong,
active, and social.

ORIENTAL
longhair and shorthair; vocal,
persistent, and affectionate.

PERSIAN (includes Himalayan)
longhair; sweet,
affectionate, and quiet.

RAGAMUFFIN
longhair; affectionate,
calm, and loves people.

RAGDOLL
longhair; affectionate,
calm, docile, and smart.

RUSSIAN BLUE
shorthair; graceful,
playful, and quiet.

SCOTTISH FOLD
longhair and shorthair;
affectionate, calm, and sweet.

SELKIRK REX
longhair and shorthair;
quiet by nature.

SIAMESE
shorthair; vocal, affectionate,
active, and persistent.

SIBERIAN
longhair; large, strong,
and determined.

SINGAPURA
shorthair; sweet, affectionate,
bossy, and demanding.

SOMALI
longhair; busy, active,
affectionate, and determined.

SPHYNX
shorthair; active
and affectionate.

TONKINESE
shorthair; social, busy, likes
humans, vocal, and loving.

TURKISH ANGORA
longhair; curious and active.

TURKISH VAN
longhair; sweet, curious
and likes water.

— CAT FACTS —

There are approximately
100 breeds of cats. For
more information go to
animal.discovery.com
or www.tica.org

the truth about shelter cats

Topics:

Living in a Shelter

Shelters provide a fascinating mix of adoptable cats.

Purebreds to one-of-a kind mixes, as well as a variety of ages can be found.

Adopting a cat from a shelter is generally less expensive than buying from a breeder or pet shop. It will also help reduce the number of cats being bred for profit.

Shelters can provide you with information on the temperament and personality of the animal, since they are handled daily by the staff and volunteers. This helps maintain the cat's sociability with humans. Some shelters also have cats living together in cat "condos" or "community cat rooms," which allow them to interact with each other. This can be beneficial when they move to a new home that has cats. There may also be current medical history or pet history from a previous guardian.

If you are looking for more than one cat, look into the cats that were brought into the shelter together or have become great pals at the shelter and adopt them together.

At the ARL and many shelters, all cats are spayed, neutered, microchipped, dewormed, and vaccinated before they are adopted.

Cats at the ARL-Iowa play and interact in the community cat room.

— CAT FACTS —

- Most pets are obtained from acquaintances and family members.

- 10 to 20 percent of cats and dogs are adopted from shelters and rescues.

(Source: Ralston Purina® and NCPPSP)

Myths About Shelter Cats

People often think that all cats in shelters were surrendered due to behavior problems. This is not true. Many of the cats in shelters have no behavior problems and the reasons for their surrender are varied. Most behavior problems are fixable, and the issue that brought the cat to the shelter may never show up in a new environment.

Do Adopted Shelter Cats Need Special Care?

Some cats in shelters can be stressed due to a sudden change from a familiar to an unfamiliar environment. They may not be used to cages and are missing the "normal" things in their life, as well as their loving owner who had to give them up. Some of these cats may need extra patience, assurance, and guidance. The staff will be able to help you with this information. But always remember that all cats will need some adjustment time, and your love and patience will pay off.

Socialization by Age Levels

To encourage good social skills in your kitten, it is important you socialize her as much as possible when she is young. This means having as many people as possible pet, play with, and hold your kitten. You want to get her used to being handled by as many people as possible. That includes picking up, brushing, petting, and playing with people other than her own humans. One great way to do this is to have friends and family visit, especially right after you get your kitten. As your kitten continues to grow, you should continue to handle her often and at different times and for different lengths of times. Also, have people touch your kitten's tail, ears and paws to get her used to being handled all over.

How Cats Learn

Like all animals, cats learn through association.

If the cat is rewarded for a behavior, he is more likely to do that same behavior in the future.

This also happens with behaviors you may have mistakenly rewarded. Actions that might have been fun or cute at first, may now pose a problem. You will need to teach a competing behavior like scratching the post and not the sofa. Remember to reward the post-scratching with high value rewards, such as a favorite treat, and the sofa scratching will fade away. The more we reward appropriate behavior, the better our cats will be.

Appropriate behavior for a cat or kitten is best described as a cat that is social and wants to be with humans. At the very least, she should never put her teeth on you, even in play. Provide entertaining activities for your cat by playing with her with Ping Pong balls, cat fishing pole toys or paper sacks. See chapter 10 for more games and enrichment activities for your cat.

Guideline for socialization

Three to eight weeks

What to expect:

Kittens' social play begins and increases steadily. They start to use the litter box, they object play, and explore climbing, running, scratching and predatory behavior.

Things you should do:

Frequent gentle handling and play with varied people including men, women, and supervised children.

Take kitten socialization classes, if available. Reward appropriate friendly behavior to humans and all other animals using treats and play. Provide litter boxes with low sides for easy entry. Make sure you provide toys and scratching posts. Teach your kitten to go into a carrier.

Never use hands and feet to play with kittens. This teaches your kitten bad habits. Always use toys.

Nine to sixteen weeks

What to expect:

At this stage, kittens continue to learn social skills, their social play peaks and there will be more vigorous exploration of the environment and climbing.

Things you should do:

Continue socializing your kittens. If they have not had previous social education, initiate slowly. They may need a larger litter box. Provide vertical space and climbing structures.

Kittens that have not had adequate social experience during early socialization may have poor social skills and require extra effort to acquire good social skills.

Seventeen weeks to one year

What to expect:

Social play will decrease. They are more likely to be subordinate to larger adults, but may also challenge these cats for status.

Things you should do:

Provide food puzzles and food toys. Make sure you continue to play with your cat and reward friendly behavior. You may want to re-evaluate the size of the litter box as well.

Guideline for socialization

One to six years

What to expect:

This is where your cat may start to slowdown, so watch for weight gain. If weight gain occurs, check with your veterinarian before changing diets. Cats mature socially at approximately two to three years, and their personality can be strongly affected by genetics and early experience.

Things you should do:

Continue to play with and reward friendly behavior. Provide your pets with enriching and entertaining activities.

If you notice any behavior changes, consult your veterinarian to ensure there is nothing medical contributing to the behavior issue. If the cat is healthy, consult a Veterinary Behaviorist or an Animal Behavior Specialist.

Behavior problems are best treated early.

Seven years and older

What to expect:

Changes in appetite can occur. Decreased activity may lead to decreased social interaction with you or other animals.

Things you should do:

Continue play and interaction with your cat. It may not be as much as it once was, but it still is important. Monitor appetite and water intake and contact your veterinarian if there are increases or decreases.

Medical problems may increase with age.

Topics:

Human-Animal Bonds

Being involved with an animal shelter for more than twenty years, I have heard thousands of stories of the special relationship humans experience with animals.

I never tire of the stories. They confirm that there are countless numbers of people everywhere who love their animals. It also tells me that the connections or bonds we have with our the animals can fulfill our lives.

It makes sense really. Pets are with you through it all—marriages and divorces, moves, new jobs and deaths in our family. They spend all the major moments of our lives with us. They listen. They never judge. After a hard day we come home to a house where a tail-wagging dog can hardly wait to greet us; or a cat runs to the door and meows a hello. They don't care what we look like or about our moods. They are just happy we are with them. We're their whole world.

Those of you who have experienced unique bonds with animals have already discovered this special relationship. For those of you who are just bringing an animal into your home, I want to share a few of my own stories.

Photo by: Kelly Kesling, Kesling Photography

First, there was my dog Freida. She came into the Animal Rescue League at a mere two weeks of age after her mother had been hit by a car. Freida came home with me so I could foster her until she was old enough to be adopted. But after bottle feeding and spending all my free time with her, we were bonded like I could never have imagined possible. Of course, I adopted her and we spent the full 16 years of her life together. When my mother died, I remember holding Freida and whispering to her. She licked my tears asking nothing of me. I knew that as long as I had her with me, I would be okay, and I meant it. Freida passed away a couple years ago and yet I think of her daily and always with the warm memory of the relationship we had.

Azzurro, a shelter cat, and I connected the minute we saw each other. Not all bonds are love at first sight; some take time to form.

Sometimes, a connection can be immediate. At the shelter I have probably met hundreds of thousands of animals in my 20 years. While we love them all, we connect on a deeper level with only a handful.

When I started volunteering at the shelter, I walked dogs and spent very little time with the cats (completely different now, of course!) —until one day— a cat caught my eye. I spent the next week not being able to get that cat out of my mind. The next week, I adopted him, my very first cat, and my life changed. Azzurro and I connected from the minute we looked at each other.

When I moved the first time, I realized the special bond. He spent the first two nights in our new home literally sleeping on top of my head (he typically never slept on the bed). It was like he had to know I was there to know he was okay in this new place. It happened when I moved a second and third time as well. Just as humans turn to animals for comfort, animals take comfort in their human families.

Bonds exist between pets that have lived together but are different species.

Birdie is very protective of Casper, her chinchilla friend.

Animal-Animal Bonds

While we talk about human bonds with our animal friends, it is just as important to mention the bonds that form between animals.

At the shelter, we have witnessed this bond between animals too many times to count. What is particularly fascinating is that bonds exist between pets that have lived together but are different species.

For example, a guinea pig and a cockatiel came into the shelter together from a family that didn't want them anymore. They were so bonded that the bird wouldn't eat unless he could see the guinea pig.

Violet and Teapot — Another such pair was a rabbit and a guinea pig. Observing how they cared for each other and the way the rabbit, Violet, protected her guinea pig friend, Teapot, was truly amazing. Anytime you approached their living quarters, Violet would step in front of Teapot, not for attention, but as if to check you out first. Once she figured out you were okay, she would step aside and allow you to pet Teapot.

Otis the Cat and Sam the Dog — As is typical at a shelter, when someone brings a dog and cat in together, the different species go to separate housing areas. With Otis and Sam, staff noticed that neither one would eat or do anything other than lie around. When we realized the situation, they were moved together to a dog kennel; and all was good with Otis and Sam.

These experiences led to a policy change. Recognizing how pets of the same or different species bond, ARL keeps the bonds intact through the ARL's "bonded buddy" adoption program. When pairs of pets – same species or not – are brought in together and are bonded, they must be adopted together and adoptive owners must sign an agreement stating they will keep them together.

Daily, my own animals demonstrate their bonds. They rub on each other; they wash each other's faces and ears. One of my cats must be in the same area as another one or he tosses a meowing fit.

Rio and Satch — Perhaps one of the strongest examples of bonding I have seen was one with my two horses, Satch and Rio. Satch is clearly the leader of my small (three) herd, but before Charlie, the third, came into our lives, it was only Rio and Satch.

Rio and Satch loved to play together with those orange construction cones. One horse would toss it up in the air; the other horse would go get it, toss it, and so on. They were separated for a week when Rio had to be in the equine vet hospital due to a sprain. When Rio came home, he had to be stall-rested for a couple of weeks. The day we brought him home and set him up in his stall; we came out an hour later to check on him. Lo and behold – there in his stall was an orange construction cone. My husband thought it was a great idea that I had placed it there; I thought he had placed it.

We quickly discovered Satch had dropped it there! Over the next few days we observed Satch getting the cone and bringing it to Rio. Rio would play with it for a bit; and then Satch would drop it in the stall for him.

I recently saw a car magnet that read "Who Rescued Whom?" It really struck home. We say we "saved" them or we "rescued" them, but when I think about it, that is only half the story. They all rescue us in one way or another. I am just one of the lucky ones that was given the gift of realizing what amazing creatures we are blessed to walk with on the Earth.

Bonds between animals are so strong, the ARL developed a Bonded Buddy program. Animals that are brought to the shelter together and are bonded must be adopted out together. Adopters are required to sign a paper stating they will keep the pets together.

My message is "Find Your Bond."

bringing your new cat or kitten home

Chapter 4

Topics:

Getting Ready for Your New Cat

Once you have decided to add a cat or kitten to your family, you need to make sure everyone in the household is prepared to have a cat or kitten and are ready to contribute to her care.

Telling a child you will get them a cat if they take care of it is not responsible or in the best interest of the cat or child. Adding a pet to the family needs to be a family decision and everyone needs to be committed to it. The cat you bring home is depending on it. Decide, or at least discuss, who will be feeding and watering the cat and who will be cleaning the litter box.

Additionally, having some knowledge about cats and their behavior is important. You will then be able to recognize when your cat is not feeling well and needs a visit to her veterinarian. Behaviorally you need to know when the cat is playing and when the cat is scared. You will need to react differently, depending on the behavior. Most people, once they have lived with their cat for a short time, will be able to read the cat's behavior.

Have Your Supplies Ready

Have the supplies you need for your cat or kitten before you get her, or get the supplies when you adopt her. Some animal shelters, including the ARL, have a pet supply store inside the shelter. It contains all the supplies you need when bringing your pet home. You will need the following to make sure your kitty feels at home:

- Collar
- Bowls for food and water
- Food
- Litter box and scoop— (see chapter 7)
- Litter—(see chapter 7)
- Toys—(see chapter 10)
- Brush or cat comb
- Scratching post
- Bed
- Nail clippers

Make sure you have the necessary supplies on hand before bringing your new cat home.

Identification and Collar

Be sure you have proper and secure identification on your cat. Even if your cat lives indoors all the time, there could be a moment when she slips out the door. You need to have a collar and identification on your cat and an implanted microchip. Most animal shelters already microchip at the time of adoption. Some give you a collar with the identification tag of the shelter, but you should add an identification tag with your name, address, and phone number in case you need to be reached. A tag is also good to have if your cat has to be at the veterinarian's office or a boarding facility overnight.

The type of collar you get is important. We recommend a "safety" or "breakaway" collar. These collars, if caught on something, will break open and allow your cat to escape. This is important inside and out, if your cat should get caught on a curtain rod or tree limb, for example. Refer to Cats and Collars on page 143.

> **We strongly caution against letting your cat outdoors.**
>
> However if you do, a safety collar, ID tag, and microchip may be what brings your cat home if she goes missing.

Acclimating Your Cat

It is interesting to observe your cat coming out of her cat carrier when you first bring her home. Is she bolting out of the carrier anxious to check things out, or does she run under the nearest couch, bed, or dresser? Cats that are scared and hesitant will need more time to acclimate to a new environment. Be sure to be patient and give them lots of love and time to adjust. Those cats that are bold will still need reassurance, love, and attention but are going acclimate in a shorter period of time. Remember every cat is different.

All cats need love and reassurance as they acclimate to their new home.

bringing your new cat or kitten home

Getting Ready for Your New Cat *Continued*

When you bring your new cat or kitten home, be sure to set up the litter box first and show your cat where it is located. If you have a kitten, put her in the litter box so she can feel the litter. If you have an adult cat, just showing her the box is enough. You do not need to put her in the litter box. Refer to Litter Training in Chapter 7.

If you have other cats or dogs, refer to Introducing a New Cat to Other Pets in Chapter 6. If you do not have other pets, allow your cat to explore. If you have a kitten, you may want to limit where she can go. You do not want her to wander too far from the litter box and forget where it is when she needs it.

Show your new cat where her litter box is located as soon as you bring her home.

Be sure you spend time with your cat as she is exploring. Be proactive in looking for things you had not considered that could hurt her or be dangerous, such as an open toilet a kitten could fall into or dangerous plants or foods left out.

Look for items lying around that she might chew on or swallow, like toilet paper, tissues, and paper towels. Pens and pencils may need to be kept in drawers. Rubber bands and hair ties can be hazardous if ingested by your cat or kitten. You may also have to secure cords to baseboards and put caps on outlets.

Make certain you put away harsh cleaning products, human medications, and household poisons. You do not want your cat to lick the outside of the containers, in case some of the liquid has dripped.

If you do not have other pets in the home, allow your cat to explore his new surroundings.

Cats need their own space, too. It is always a good idea when bringing new pets home to set them up with an area or room that is theirs—for food and a litter box. These items should not be next to each other, but be spaced a few feet apart or across the room from each other. The area should be a low-traffic room that kids and other pets don't frequent. This will be your cat's safe space to sniff, eat, scratch, and play while she gets her bearings. Arrange her food and water bowls, bed and litter box in different areas of the room. The food and water should not be next to the litter box or the bed. Scatter her toys around. You can even clean off a windowsill for her and have soft music playing. She will appreciate the chance to feel out her new family from inside her haven.

Give her time alone in her room to get comfortable before you come in to play with her. Then, visit her often and let her out to explore and run around if there are not other pets in the home. If there are other pets in the home, see chapter 6 to learn how to introduce your pets. With a whole new life in store for her, your cat will need some time and space to check out her surroundings and all her new play things.

Give your new cat her own space with food and litter box. She will soon be comfortable in her new surroundings and be ready to explore.

Your cat should be checked by your veterinarian within a few days of adoption. If you do not have a vet, refer to chapter 5, Choosing a Veterinarian.

Getting Ready for Your New Cat *Continued*

Visit the veterinarian within the first few days. It is important you take your new cat to the veterinarian in the first few days so he can get a baseline of your pet right away. Most shelters will provide you with a health assessment form you can share with your vet so he is aware of your cat's history in terms of vaccination, spaying/neutering and microchipping before adoption. You may want to make this appointment even before you bring your kitten home. Maintain veterinary records for the life of your cat and be sure to provide your pet with regular and necessary veterinary medical care.

Cats like structure. Be sure to keep your new pet's life as structured as possible in the first days and weeks. Leave the litter box where you had it unless you absolutely have to move it. Feed the same food and use the same litter so the scent and feel on your cat's paws are the same. If necessary, make changes later, after you have established a bond and relationship with your cat.

Allow your new cat some alone time. She will appreciate it as she acclimates to her new family.

Feeding Your New Cat

"How do I feed my new cat or kitten?" is a common question among new cat owners. You may wonder what to feed, how much to feed, and how often to feed your cat. Cats have different needs, so having a conversation with your veterinarian about your cat's dietary needs is an important one.

When you adopt a cat, ask the shelter what your cat has been eating. Most shelters use donated food so your cat's diet may be varied. If you are changing your cat's diet, you will want to do a mix for a time with the food the cat is used to eating and the food you are going to be feeding. Lessen the amount of "old" food the cat was eating every few days, until you are only feeding the new food. This will decrease the likelihood of diarrhea.

Whether you feed your cat dry, canned, or semi-moist food, be sure to purchase a high quality product recommended by your veterinarian. You can then be assured your cat is receiving an adequate supply of vitamins and minerals. Do not add any vitamin or mineral supplements without a veterinarian's approval. This may actually harm your cat.

Most cats are comfortable with what we call "free feeding". This means food is left out and available to them at all times. However, if you have an overweight cat or a cat with specific medical needs, you may need to feed a more restricted diet. This also means you will need to feed your cat at specific times during the day and evening.

Most cats do well with having food available to them at all times.

Teach your child to support the cat's hindquarters and chest when picking him up.

Supervise your child and pet whenever they are together.

Do not allow your child to disturb her pet when he is sleeping.

How Kids Should Handle Cats or Kittens

Anyone who has grown up with a cat or kitten, knows what a great experience it is. Pets can be our best friends after a tough day at school or after a teenage heartbreak.

Bringing a new cat or kitten home is an exciting thing, especially for kids. It is important you ensure your children are handling their new pet in a humane and compassionate manner.

Tips for fostering a great relationship between kids and pets

• **Teach children how to handle a cat properly.** To pick up a cat, support the cat's hindquarters in one hand and use the other to support her chest. Hold the cat gently and securely close to your body. Cats should not be picked up by the scruff of the neck. Never allow kids to pull the cat's tail or whiskers or to poke at her. If your kids are too young to responsibly pick up the cat, teach them not to pick her up but to pet her gently and slowly instead.

• **Supervise kids and cats.** Supervision is especially important with a new pet. Teach children to respect the cat and do not allow them to chase or corner her, even in play. The cat may bite if she feels threatened. Encourage calm, non-threatening interactions. If your kids cannot be calm and gentle, allow the cat an "escape route" into another room. For example, put a baby gate across a door with six-inches open underneath or a cat tree where they can get up high. This will allow your cat to escape under the gate or up the cat tree but limit your child's access to the room.

How Kids Should Handle Cats or Kittens *Continued*

• **Do not allow children to disturb a sleeping or eating cat.** Also give her some space when she is using her litter box. Tell your children that when the cat is sleeping, using her litter box, or eating, they should not bother the cat.

• **Do not allow rough play.** Rough play encourages your cat to use her teeth and claws on you. Play with your cat using commercial cat toys or those you have made. For example, many cats love to play in a simple paper bag. Toys such as Ping-Pong balls or something soft that can be tossed by your kids for the cat to chase are great. Refer to Cat Toys and How to Use Them in Chapter 10

• **Do not allow children to tease the cat.** Teach kids the difference between teasing and playing. Never allow your kids to tease any pet.

• **Teach children how important it is to keep your cat indoors.** Help children understand the importance of keeping their pet safe. Teach them to watch the cat when the door is open so she does not accidentally run out the door.

Share the responsibility of caring for your cat with your children.

Never expect your young child to assume all responsibility for a pet.

If there are issues with your pet, seek help from a pet behavior specialist.

Your child will learn that you don't give up on a family member, but instead, you work it out.

Even though your cat is not allowed outdoors, she will enjoy watching birds and other activities from a safe perch inside.

Topics:

Choosing a Veterinarian

Having a veterinarian for your furry family members is as important as having a good medical doctor for the humans in the household.

It is important to establish a good relationship with a veterinarian you like and trust for your pet. Ask friends for a recommendation, and make an appointment to meet with a veterinarian to ensure you feel comfortable, just as you would with any other doctor. Choose a vet with whom you are comfortable and who will answer your questions.

Be sure to observe the office itself when you first visit a veterinarian's office. Observe the demeanor of the office staff and those working with the animal patients. Do you feel they are kind and compassionate? Would you want them handling your pet?

Another way to find a veterinarian you can feel good about is to ask your local animal shelter or humane society if there are any veterinarians volunteering their time or services to help at the shelter.

24-Hour Emergency Care

Hopefully, you will never need it, but it is important to have 24-hour emergency care available. Ask your veterinarian for an emergency care plan and to give you the number of a 24-hour emergency veterinary facility in your area. Keep this number on your refrigerator and check with your vet when you visit to be sure it is still up-to-date.

The health and well-being of your cat depends on you. Make sure to keep his vaccinations current and take him to see your veterinarian annually.

First Visit to the Veterinarian

The shelter you adopt your cat from will most likely provide you with a health record which will contain all the vaccinations and other health-related information you need. Take this information to your veterinarian at your cat's first visit. If you do not receive a health record from the shelter, ask about prior vaccinations, nutrition, parasite control, microchips, spaying or neutering, grooming and any tests that were run, such as feline leukemia virus and feline immunodeficiency virus.

Take your new cat to a veterinarian as soon as possible. If you have other cats at home, and especially if the newcomer's health history is not known, keep the new cat separated from your other cats until your veterinarian has had a chance to examine him.

If no health history is available, your veterinarian will likely run a few tests to determine that your new cat is free from disease. One of the first tests may be for feline leukemia virus (FeLV) and feline immunodeficiency virus (FIV). FeLV and FIV weaken the immune system, leaving the cat vulnerable to secondary infections and cancer.

In addition to testing for these diseases, your veterinarian will also likely analyze a fecal sample to test for intestinal parasites. Even if your new cat has had previous stool samples examined, it is important to keep in mind they are only snapshots in time of parasite life cycles, and one sample may not reveal all parasites. Having repeat fecal exams is important, especially in kittens. Intestinal parasites deprive the infected cat of important nutrition, causing weakness and susceptibility to viral or bacterial infections. Keeping your cat free of parasites is important for her long-term health.

Your veterinarian will check your cat's

heart and lungs

teeth

First Visit to the Veterinarian *Continued*

Your veterinarian will check your cat's

fur and skin for external parasites

ears

Once in a while, an owner may see an intestinal parasite that resembles a white threadlike worm or a rice grain near the cat's tail. This is a treatable medical condition. If your cat is infected, proper medication should be obtained from your veterinarian and a fecal sample should be checked after treatment to ensure the parasites have been eliminated.

During the physical examination, your veterinarian will also check your cat for external parasites, such as fleas, ticks and mites. External parasites are the cause of most common skin disorders and can transmit other diseases, such as Lyme disease. Your veterinarian can provide effective treatments and control methods for your cat's external parasites.

Upper respiratory tract viruses are extremely common in cats. They are like a head cold and you may see this in a cat you adopt from a shelter. Most shelters are dealing with hundreds of cats, and just like a child in a classroom, colds spread easily. Most common respiratory viruses will run their course with little treatment as long as a secondary bacterial infection does not cause complications. Make sure your cat is hydrated, eating well and has a place to rest. Other viruses, however, may require more extensive treatment. Your veterinarian can guide you through whether or not treatment is needed.

Preventive Measures

Your veterinarian can give you advice on your cat's nutrition. They can also provide yearly physical examinations to assess the overall health of your cat.

Adopting. If you adopt from a shelter, most cats will have already been spayed or neutered, implanted with a microchip and provided some vaccinations and wormer. The shelter will give you a health record you can take to your veterinarian.

Feline Vaccination Schedule

A series of vaccines for kittens and regularly scheduled vaccines for adult cats are one of the best ways to ensure your cat is protected from deadly infectious feline diseases.

We recommend a feline distemper vaccination, a feline leukemia vaccination, and a feline rabies vaccination for all cats. These illnesses are the most common feline diseases. They often prove deadly to cats of all ages, but are especially dangerous for kittens. Your kitten should begin to receive vaccines against these diseases at approximately six weeks of age, once the maternal antibodies from his mother's milk have begun to lose their protectiveness.

Following the initial vaccination series, your maturing cat will require a booster set of vaccinations every one to three years depending on vaccine type and local ordinances. These additional vaccinations are necessary to keep your pet's immune system ready to fight off disease.

The rabies vaccination is required by law in many cities and counties. The vaccine should be given when the cat is eight-to twelve-weeks old, depending on the vaccine type, and then one year later. The vaccine should be given every one to three years after this, depending on the vaccine type and the local rabies-vaccination requirements. If you adopt a mature cat and are unsure of the rabies vaccination history, you will need to get your cat vaccinated as if it were of kitten age to ensure your cat is protected.

Risks of Vaccinations

Vaccines may produce some negative side effects.

Typically, the following mild reactions are common following a vaccination:

- Inflammation or swelling around the spot of injection
- Lethargy
- Loss of appetite
- Fever

Rarely, a cat may experience a severe reaction to a vaccination:

- Lump or swelling around the site of the injection that does not go away within a few days
- Signs of an allergic reaction

Contact your veterinarian immediately as these may be signs of a severe and potentially life-threatening reaction to the vaccination.

Keep proper records of your cat's vaccinations, and speak with your veterinarian if you have any questions or concerns.

Determining Which Vaccines Your Cat Should Receive

How do you know which vaccinations to give your cat or kitten?

Ask your veterinarian. Even looking on the Internet, there are different answers to different questions on frequency and type of vaccinations necessary. This is another reason why it is important to have a veterinarian you trust.

Things to consider when deciding which vaccinations to give:

- The likelihood your cat will contract certain diseases, including risk factors such as your location, her diet and other cats in the area

- The severity of the disease

- The overall success rate and side effects of the vaccine

- Your cat's health and disease history

Feline Vaccination Schedule *Continued*

The most-common combination vaccine, usually called FVRCP, protects your cat against three diseases: feline panleukopenia, feline viral rhinotracheitis, and disease caused by feline calicivirus. Feline panleukopenia, also called feline distemper, is a highly contagious and deadly viral disease in cats.

Generally, the first FVRCP vaccination is given when your cat is six to eight weeks old. The vaccine is then repeated at three- to four-week intervals until the kitten is sixteen weeks old. After this initial vaccination series, boosters are given one year later and then every three years, to keep the cat protected.

An adult cat that is adopted without a health history would receive two vaccination boosters three to four weeks apart. The initial vaccination series should be boosted one year later and then every three years, according to the American Association of Feline Practitioners guidelines.

If you have adopted an adult cat without a rabies vaccination history, she will need to begin the vaccination schedule as if she were a kitten.

Some happy endings
from the Animal Rescue League of Iowa

Gus and Fiona

Gone to a
Good Home!

Ziggy and Delia

Gus, Fiona, Ziggy, Delia and Pretty Mama

We found four kittens, Gus, Fiona, Ziggy, and Delia, in a nest in the bushes on a Friday afternoon outside Landauer Publishing. We didn't know if they had been abandoned or if their mother was a feral cat in hiding. I called my vet and the Animal Rescue League. They said, "Don't leave the kittens outside."

The kittens seemed healthy. Their eyes were open and they were very mobile. I volunteered to take the kittens home over the weekend and feed them every three hours as instructed.

Monday, I took them to my vet who told me the kittens were 3-1/2 weeks old, weighing 10-12 ounces. My vet gave me advice on care and feeding. Determined to raise them to good heath and find them homes, I went back to the office where I would continue their care.

Within an hour of returning to work with four little kittens, my vet called to say, "We have a mother cat nursing 4 kittens here. Bring your kittens back to see if this mother cat will accept and nurse them, too."

'Pretty Mama' was laid on a table and presented with the four tiny kittens. With barely a sound, she let the kittens nurse immediately. The vet offered to let the kittens stay with Pretty Mama. The kittens flourished, nursed and cared for by a mother cat, which is always the best way to raise kittens.

Five weeks later, after the kittens were weaned, spayed and neutered, they all needed homes. We kept two, Gus and Fiona, at Landauer. I found a home for the other two, Ziggy and Delia, with my neighbor, Jean. Pretty Mama went home with my friend, Carol. Vet staff and clients adopted Mama's four kittens.

In all, Pretty Mama and eight kittens found happy, forever homes.

Sue

Pretty Mama

introducing a new cat to other pets

Topics:

Introducing a New Cat to Other Family Cats

Introducing your new cat to other cats in your home can be a tricky process.

However, it is one of the most important things to do correctly with your cat or kitten.

Take your new cat into your home in a cat carrier. Many shelters, including the Animal Rescue League, provide you with a cardboard carrier when you adopt a pet.

Confine

Immediately confine the newcomer to one room with a litter box, food, water and bed. Leave the cat separated from other pets in the home for a few days. The biggest mistake you can make in building relationships between your resident cat and a newcomer is to let the newcomer roam through the house immediately after coming home. Patience is absolutely key in building a lasting relationship between the cats. Go in and visit your new cat, play with him, pet him, feed him and make him feel that this is now home. Remember your cat is probably confused and frightened. You need to reassure him all is well. Leaving a TV or radio on is a good way to give your cat some background noise.

Introduce your new cat and resident cat gradually. This will help them build a positive, lasting relationship.

Scent

Scent is absolutely critical to getting cats used to each other. During the separation time, take a bath towel and rub it on your new cat as if you are trying to dry him off. Take the same towel and rub it on the resident cat. Leave that towel in your living room or around the house where your resident cat hangs out. You are taking the scent of your new cat and putting it on the resident one. Take a second towel and repeat the procedure, beginning with your resident cat. Leave that towel in the room with your newcomer cat.

By doing this exercise every day, you are getting the cats' scents onto each other. When they meet face to face, they will smell familiar.

You can escalate the procedure by taking cooking vanilla and dabbing it on the base of their tails, where they can't lick. It cements the scent issue, making the cats smell the same scent—vanilla. Do this every other day.

Scent is key when introducing a new cat and resident cat.

Vanilla on the base of each cat's tail will familiarize your cats with the same scent before they meet.

Introducing a New Cat to Other Family Cats *Continued*

A successful way to build a good relationship between the cats is to reward them when they are in the same room or proximity and behaving appropriately.

They don't need to love each other from day one, but they do need to be able to be in the same room without warfare. If they are in the same room and involved in an activity without behavior problems, give them treats and tell them "good kitties" in a soft voice. You can also take a fishing pole toy and play with them together, as this will be a fun activity for both of them.

Switch

After a time, switch the cats. Take the newcomer cat and place him in the rest of the house. Put your resident cat in the room where you had sequestered the newcomer. The newcomer can explore his new surroundings and spread his scent around the house. This allows both animals to become used to the scent of the other before actual face-to-face contact. This process may take a few hours or a few days, depending on how the cats react. Start with a couple areas and then switch back. Repeat the procedure the next day.

Introduction

After a few days, it is time for an introduction. Do this when you are going to be home. Do not leave the cats together unsupervised for a period of time after the initial introduction. Open the door to the sequestered room and allow the cat to come out on his own and explore. Allow the cats to meet each other on their own terms.

You can also use a baby gate across the door to the sequestered room and allow the cats to meet with the baby gate between them for the first few times. This is a good device when you are uncertain how the introduction will go.

If you feed meals at a set time of the day, this is a good time for face-to-face introductions. They will be so busy eating they won't have time for fighting. Be sure to give each cat his own bowl on opposite sides of the room. Make it a special dinner with great smelling food.

Avoid forcing a meeting between your cats. This may cause unnecessary fighting. Let them get acquainted gradually to help develop a positive relationship. This will lessen any territorial problems.

Expect hissing, spitting and growling. Do not interfere, unless an actual fight breaks out. If this happens, throw a blanket over each cat and confine them to different quarters. Keep them separated until they have calmed down. Then start over.

By allowing your cats to get acquainted gradually you are increasing the chances that they will form a positive relationship.

Introducing a New Cat to the Family Dog

When bringing a new cat into a household with a dog, the introduction should be a positive experience for all involved. The introduction is similar to when a cat is already in the home. It is best to have a slow, gradual introduction with gradual exposure to each other.

When the time comes for the cat and dog to meet, it should be done slowly and under control. When you allow the cat to roam, your dog should be under control and not allowed to chase or harass the cat. This can be accomplished by having your dog on a leash. This ensures your cat is safe and you can teach your dog how you would like him to behave around the cat.

The most important thing to teach your dog and reward him for is staying calm. Your dog will also learn that when the cat is present, he gets treats. This will build a positive association of the cat for your dog. When you feel your dog understands how you would like him to act, let the dog greet the cat slowly. Leave the leash on the dog in case you have to grab him in a hurry.

Make sure your cat has places where she can escape and get up high to feel safe, especially if your dog tries to chase her.

Determine what your new cat likes in the way of treats and play. When the cat is near the dog, reward her with her favorite treat or play a favorite game.

Provide places for your cat to escape and feel safe in case your dog tries to chase her.

Do not let your pets meet and sort it out.

This could go very wrong, and even if neither gets hurt, they will probably never get along.

Never leave your dog and cat alone unless you can guarantee one hundred percent nothing will happen.

Introducing a New Cat to the Family Bird

An important factor to remember when introducing your new cat to the family bird is genetic makeup. Your cat is a predator. The genetic makeup of your bird is to be prey. With that in mind, placement of the bird's cage will depend on the type of bird and cage set-up you have.

Small or hanging bird cages should be placed away from any object the cat could use to jump onto the cage. All perches should be placed in the middle of the cage. This way the bird can sit on the perch and the cat cannot make contact with the bird.

Your cat should not be allowed to stalk or harass your bird. You may want to have a place in the cage where your bird can hide and feel safe. You can also place a skirt around the bottom portion of the cage to block the cat's view of the bird.

Prevent your cat from harassing the bird by blocking her view with a skirt around the bottom of the cage.

Some happy endings
from the Animal Rescue League of Iowa

Spice and Sugar

I adopted two 3-month old kittens from ARL West. They have already made themselves at home and are learning the rules very quickly. Sugar (the tiger) is absolutely fearless and is already playing with the dog, Merry (also an adoptee). Spice (the calico) is a little more cautious, but is getting used to Merry. Both kittens love to snuggle.

Rebecca

Ziggy and Carmella

When I went to the ARL fashion show event, I was a little worried that I'd want to bring home another small dog; I have a miniature dachshund. However, the big, longhaired cats really caught my eye. I thought seriously about adopting a Ragdoll cat but Carmella's coloring was just so pretty. I couldn't bear the thought that Ziggy and Carmella might have a hard time finding a home because they needed to stay together. I decided I had plenty of room in my house and my heart for two. It is ironic that I chose Carmella because she is so pretty, when it is Ziggy who has really stolen our hearts. Carmella's a bit reserved and shy. She's not skittish or fearful, and I think she'll become more outgoing once she's more settled. Ziggy, however, lives to eat and be petted. Strangers are all just friends he hasn't yet met. He spends his nights alternating between my bed and my daughter's. Whomever he can wake up to give him a good scratch behind the ears gets the pleasure of his company. I have a feeling I will eventually turn into the little old lady in the rocker with Carmella on my lap in front of the fire while Ziggy, Katie (my daughter) and Roxie (my dog) rule the rest of the house. They are great cats and I can't fathom why their previous parents would move out of state and not take them along.

Marce

litter training

With any luck at all, the mother cat has given your new kitten some sound litter box training. Even though a kitten is more energetic than an older cat, she is not as rigidly set in her ways and will be more open to training. An untrained older cat might require a little more patience on your part.

Choosing the Right Litter Box

Choosing the correct litter box for your cat is important. If you adopt a cat from a shelter, the staff should be able to provide some insight as to what kind of litter they have been using as well as the type of litter box (covered, uncovered, liners or no liners). You also need to keep in mind the size of your cat. A litter box that is too small may cause issues and your cat will stop using it. Your cat should be able to easily get in the box, use it and turn around to cover up his waste. If you adopt a kitten, you can start with a small box, but remember to upgrade it as the cat grows. The larger litter box should be the same texture and design when you upgrade.

While some cats use covered boxes for years without any problems, they can be a common source of litter box issues. If possible, use an open box with no cover. If you are unsure, you may want to provide a covered and uncovered litter box and see which one your cat prefers.

Keep in mind that as your cat ages you may need to change litter box styles. If the cat has always used a covered litter pan, a change in body composition or mobility may make removing the cover important. If a cat has become overweight, she may no longer fit comfortably in a covered box. An older cat with musculoskeletal changes, such as arthritis, may find climbing into an uncovered box, or a litter box with lower sides, much easier.

After a bit of trial and error, your cat will let you know which litter and style of litter box she prefers.

Choice and Depth of Litter

The choice of litter material is important. Some cats prefer a plain clay litter material without any odor control added. Other cats may prefer fine clay litter materials that clump and allow for frequent and easy litter box cleaning. It is best to duplicate the type of litter that was being used at the shelter, since your cat is already used to it.

Note that litters with perfumes or additives may cause your cat to rebel. Some cats have an aversion to these scents.

Generally, most cats prefer litter at least two inches deep. This will help them cover what they have done earlier in the day and give them something to go in later in the day before the box has been cleaned with a scoop. Your cats will let you know if you don't get it right.

Types of Litter

Clumpable/scoopable litter can be used to give your cat something softer to use.

We recommend clay or clumpable litter but to see which litter your cat is most likely to use, place a box with clumpable/scoopable litter next to a box with another type of litter. See which litter your cat prefers.

Examples of various litters are shown.

100% Whole Kernel Corn Litter

Clay Litter with/without Odor Control

Corn Fiber and Baking Soda Litter

Covered Pans

Covered pans may hold in odors that are associated with infrequent cleaning.

We receive several calls about litter box issues. If the litter box has a cover on it, we suggest removing the cover and that usually solves the problem.

There is also an issue we call "escape route syndrome" that is sometimes common in cats living in households with other cats, pets, kids or a lot of activity. Some cats develop a fear of going into a covered box and not being able to see what is coming from one direction or another. There is only one escape route to that cat—and it is out the one door of the covered box. If a cat is fearful about all the activity, he may feel like he would be trapped if he goes in to use the box, and so chooses not to use it. Removing the cover will immediately solve this problem.

Mewsings
Which Cat?

Determining Which Cat Is the Culprit

Question: "I have multiple cats. One of them is not using the litter box. How can I tell which one is soiling?"

Answer: Confinement of one or more of the cats may be necessary to discover which one is not using the litter box. A video camera may also be set up and pointed at the litter boxes to assess the situation. A special dye can be administered to one cat and the soiled areas can then be evaluated with a special light. This will determine if that cat is the culprit.

Setting Up the Litter Box

Location, Location, Location

As you set up the litter box, find a spot where you are comfortable leaving the box for an extended period of time. Moving the box from place to place can cause a cat, and especially a kitten, confusion as to where she is supposed to be going. The location should be easily accessible and offer your cat privacy. Do not place your cat's litter box in a high traffic area or near the noisy washing machine. You also do not want to place it in a dark hallway or closet area. The litter box should be set up so the cat can use it and "escape" out a door if she chooses.

If there are multiple cats in the home, multiple litter boxes in several locations may be needed. It is speculated that cats do not share space equally, and may be unwilling to go to some locations to use the litter box.

Show your adult cat the box. Do not put him in the box. If you have a kitten, place him in the box so he feels the litter. Make sure you have more than one litter box, if you have a multi-level house. Kittens are like children and sometimes the urge to go hits them without warning, so it is important to have easy access to a box.

Using Cat Box Liners

Some cats don't mind liners in the litter box. Others absolutely hate them and will refuse to use a litter box with liners. Experiment to see if your cat is bothered by a liner in the box. Make sure the liner is fixed in place, so your cat doesn't get caught in it.

Covered litter box

Litter Box Maintenance

Litter box maintenance refers to how the box is cleaned. For some cats, it is necessary to keep the litter box scrupulously clean. This may mean changing the box daily or at least removing feces every day.

You should scoop the litter box daily and clean it completely twice a week. Even if the litter is clumpable, the box should be totally cleaned out and washed with hot soapy water. Cats may be reluctant to use the litter box if it has recently been deodorized or if the cat dislikes the odor of the cleansers, so rinse well after cleaning. Do not use bleach to clean the litter box, as the smell is just too strong.

Keep in mind that cleaning the litter box too often, especially if you are dealing with a kitten, may set up expectations as an adult that the box will be cleaned after every use. The same can be said for not cleaning it often enough.

An uncovered litter box and litter scoops are shown. You may also use storage containers as an alternative to a larger litter box.

House Soiling—
Determining the Behavioral Cause

When all medical problems have been treated or ruled out and the house soiling persists, a complete and comprehensive behavioral history is necessary in order to establish a diagnosis and treatment plan.

This includes:

- Information about the home environment.

- Litter box type and litter used.

- Litter box maintenance and placement.

- The onset, frequency, duration and progression of problem elimination behaviors.

- New pets in the household.

- Any household changes that might have occurred around the time the problem began.

- Any patterns to the elimination such as time of day, particular days of the week or seasonal variations.

- Relationships between the soiling cat and other animals and people in the home.

- The cat's use of the litter box at all, and the location of inappropriate elimination, including types of surface, horizontal or vertical surfaces, and whether it is urine, stools or both.

Dealing with Problem Behaviors

Feline inappropriate elimination is the most common behavioral complaint of kitten and cat owners. Problem behaviors can include urine or stool deposited outside the litter box, or marking behaviors, such as spraying or horizontal urination. Inappropriate elimination can be solved fairly easily, if the owner is willing to make the small changes necessary.

Physical Examination

A complete physical examination, urinalysis, and, in some cases, additional diagnostic tests will be needed to rule out medical problems that could be contributing to the cat's elimination problems. Some problems may be transient or recurrent so repeated tests may be needed to diagnose the problem.

Medical Reasons for House Soiling

Medical diseases of the urinary tract can cause inappropriate elimination.

- Stones and crystal formation in the bladder, bacterial infections, and a group of inflammatory diseases of the bladder and urinary tract of unknown origin can cause pain and an increased urgency to urinate.

- Diseases of the kidneys and liver can cause the cat to drink more and urinate more frequently.

- Age-related brain function decline and endocrine disorders, such as hyperthyroidism and diabetes, can lead to changes in elimination habits, including house soiling.

Dealing with Problem Behaviors *Continued*

- The pet's mobility and sensory function should also be considered. Medical conditions affecting the nerves, muscles or joints could lead to enough discomfort, stiffness, or weakness that the cat may not be able to get to the litter box, climb into it, or get into a comfortable position for elimination. If elimination is associated with pain or discomfort or if access to the litter box is uncomfortable or difficult, the cat may begin to eliminate outside of the box.

Medical problems that lead to discomfort or difficulty in passing stools, poor control or an increased frequency of defecation could contribute to house soiling with stools. Colitis, constipation, and anal sac diseases are just a few of the medical problems that need to be ruled out when diagnosing the cause of inappropriate defecation.

In addition, cats with increased frequency of elimination and those with decreased control may begin to soil the house.

Defecation issues

Much of the information needed for a urination problem is needed to make a diagnosis in defecation problems. After medical problems have been ruled out, the same diagnostic and treatment considerations as in urine house soiling will need to be considered. Defecation is typically quicker to solve than urination. But remember, both can be solved.

Non-Medical Reasons for House Soiling

Diagnostic possibilities for elimination problems in cats include litter, litter box, location and the type of flooring (substrate) under the box.

Frustration or stress can also influence feline elimination behavior. When frustration, stress, anxiety or marking are suspected to be the cause, behavior modification techniques are most often effective.

Mewsings
UTI Infection

New Litter Box and Litter

Question: "I took my cat, Pumpkin, to the veterinarian when she started having litter box issues. She had a urinary tract infection (UTI) and with medication, it cleared up. For some reason, Pumpkin still won't use her litter box. She is a five-year-old, spayed female and had never had a UTI before."

Answer: Pumpkin had associated the burning, tingling pain of her UTI with the litter box. She is using the litter box to urinate and the sensation from the infection causes a bad feeling. A lot of times a cat thinks the litter box caused the issue. To get Pumpkin back to using the litter box, you need to change the box just a little so she thinks it is new. When she uses it, she won't have the same feeling because the UTI has been cleared up.

You can do this by changing the size of the box or the litter. I recommend putting a second box by the old box and putting in a different kind of cat litter. I typically only recommend two kinds of litter—regular clay or clumpable. So if the old box has clumpable litter in it, put clay in the new one or vice versa. Let Pumpkin see the new box being set up with new litter. Curiosity will get her in the box, and she will feel differently. She will use it and think all is well with the world again.

Dealing with Problem Behaviors *Continued*

Litter box location

If your cat is eliminating only on carpet or wood flooring it can indicate a substrate (flooring) preference. You may need to offer other litter choices.

For cats that show a clear location preference for their accidents, placing a litter box in the location where they eliminate may help. If the cat uses the box in that location, it should be left there for one week. Then the box can slowly be moved to a new location that is somewhat identical in setup as the place the cat was inappropriately going. This needs to be done carefully to be sure the cat follows the box and continues to eliminate in the litter box as it is moved. Most importantly, the box should be moved only six to twelve inches at a time. It should be left in each place at least one day. When going from one room to another, or up or down stairs, longer distances can be covered as long as the cat follows the box and continues to use it.

Problem: If your cat is eliminating on a particular surface type, such as carpeting or tiled floors, it may indicate a substrate preference.

Solution: If it is happening in only one or two places, the cat should be prevented from being in that location without supervision. You should always know where the cat is when you are home. This can be accomplished by using a bell on an approved collar. In some cases, access to the problem area can be permanently prevented by closing doors, putting up barricades, or confining the cat away from the area.

The surface can be made less appealing by its texture. Remove the carpeting or make the surface uncomfortable with double-sided tape or a plastic carpet runner with the nubs up. The appeal of the surface can also be reduced by eliminating all odors that might be attracting the cat back to the area. Do this by cleaning and applying commercial odor neutralizers. Sometimes changing the function of the area may reduce the cat's desire to eliminate in that space.

Cleaning Supplies That Work for Accidents

Nature's Miracle® is a great cleaning agent for pet accidents that occur on your carpet. It is available at any pet supply store.

Type of Litter

For cats that prefer to eliminate on only one type of substrate, such as a wood floor or carpet, offer other litter choices. Some cats may prefer a clumping litter, cedar shavings or recycled newspaper. For cats that prefer solid or hard surfaces, an empty litter box or one with minimal litter might work. A carpeted ledge around the box or some discarded or shredded carpet can help increase the appeal for cats that prefer to eliminate on carpets. Some potting soil or a mixture of sand and soil may be preferable for cats that eliminate in plants or soil.

It may require a little imagination to determine what your cat prefers. Your choice should be based on the type of surfaces in the home on which the cat is eliminating.

Changing Type of Litter Gradually

If your cat was using her litter box and then you decided to change the litter to something "better," you may have a problem.

If for some reason you have to change cat litters, gradually mix the new litter you are switching to with the litter you are currently using. Do this over a period of time, slowly increasing the amount of new litter you are adding until it is completely switched.

It is important to note that most cats will never have a litter box problem. The small percentage that do can be worked with to get them back in the box.

Mewsings
A Stable Location

Pick a Spot and Leave It

Question: "I just adopted, Stephen, an eight-week-old kitten and I'm already in love with him. I'm not sure what to do, he peed in the living room instead of his litter box."

Answer: As our conversation went on, it turned out Stephen's owner had been unable to decide where to put the litter box and had moved it eleven times in 24 hours. He assumed his kitten would just know where it was and use it.

Kittens are like little kids. They can't hold it for long periods of time while they are hunting for their litter box, so you must leave the box in one spot.

Litter Box Issues

Litter box problems can be solved. It may take time and some adjustments in the home, but they can be solved. Too many cats are turned into animal shelters every year for "litter box issues" that were solvable. Pet owners need patience and to be committed to solving the problem.

If litter problems persist, you may need to confine your cat away from the area she has soiled while figuring out the situation.

Dealing with Problem Behaviors *Continued*

Problems Persist—What Next?

Once in a while, even after making the litter area more appealing and decreasing the appeal of the soiled areas, the problem persists.

Confining your cat to an area away from those that have been soiled is often necessary to re-establish litter box use. Generally, a small room such as a laundry room, extra bathroom or bedroom where the cat has not previously soiled should be utilized. Make sure your cat has bedding, food, water and a litter box. Confine your pet in an area where the litter box and litter area are appealing with no obvious deterrents or surfaces the cat is likely to soil.

In rare cases where the cat will not use the litter box at all, confinement in a cage with a floor pan covered in litter and a ledge for perching and sleeping may be needed to get litter box use restarted. Most cats will require confinement to this area for one to four weeks. The longer the problem has existed, the longer the confinement period will need to be to establish good litter use.

Confinement, however, may not be required all of the time. For example, if the cat only eliminates out of his box at night, or when the owners are preparing for work, then these are the only times the cat may need to be confined. Many cats, when supervised, will not eliminate in inappropriate areas. These cats can be allowed out of confinement when the owner is available to supervise.

It may also be possible to allow cats out of confinement with minimal supervision for the first few hours after the cat has eliminated in its litter box. Allowing release from confinement and some food treats immediately following elimination may also serve to reward use of the litter box. Over time, cats that have been confined should be given more freedom and less supervision.

Treating for Elimination Problems

To establish regular litter box usage, treatment focuses on modifying the environment and the cat's behavior.

- Prevent or deter the cat from returning to the soiled areas.

- If there is an anxiety or marking component, drugs may be useful along with behavior modification.

Trials may be helpful to determine the cat's preferences.

- Litter trials - using two or more litter types.

- Location trials - using two or more litter box locations.

- Litter box trials - using two or more styles of litter boxes.

A Monstrous Trauma

Monster in the Basement

Question: "My five-year-old cat Baxter has always used the litter box in the basement until recently. Now every morning— and only in the morning—Baxter urinates at the top of the basement stairs."

Answer: A home visit showed Baxter's litter box was right next to the hot water heater. Every morning when the family was getting ready for work and taking showers, the hot water heater made loud clanging noises. Baxter was scared to go to the basement to use his box when there was a "monster" right next to it. We moved the litter box across the basement and, since the water heater was old and needed replacing, Baxter's owner got a new one. Baxter was quickly back to using his box.

Most cats know to use their boxes, and they want to. But in Baxter's case, fear kept him from it. We need to think in their terms, not ours.

Dealing with Problem Behaviors *Continued*

Using Drugs to Treat Problems

While we only recommend non-drug behavior modification, drug therapy can be helpful where stress, anxiety, marking or a medical component is involved. An accurate diagnosis is needed to determine if such therapy will be helpful and which drug to choose will be determined by your veterinarian or a veterinarian behaviorist.

If the behavior is due to a surface substrate preference, location preference or any type of aversion, drug therapy is unlikely to be helpful. Commonly used drugs include buspirone, anti-depressants and benzodiazepines. You can medicate your cat and the problem may subside for a period of time, but unless you figure out what is causing your cat to avoid using the litter box, the problem will resurface. All drugs have the potential for side effects, some can be serious. They can also change your cat's personality. The best thing to do is work to solve the environmental and behavioral problems without drug use.

Reasons Your Cat May Have Quit Using the Litter Box

- Medical problems
- Location of litter box
- Unclean box
- Litter choice
- Litter box size
- Privacy issues
- Number of cats compared to number of litter boxes
- Moving location of litter box
- Other pets or activity in litter box area or territory

If Nothing Is Working

If your cat isn't using the litter box, you want to get help as soon as possible. Talk to your veterinarian to make sure there is not a medical condition. Once your kitten or cat has been cleared medically, consult your veterinarian or an experienced behavior specialist that uses only positive behavior modification techniques.

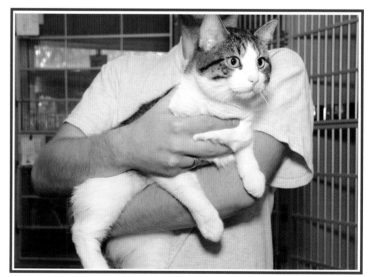

Consult your veterinarian first to make sure a medical condition isn't contributing to your cat's litter box issues.

What Not To Do

Cats do NOT do things out of anger.

They are trying to communicate there is a problem.
If you punish your cat when she doesn't use her litter box,
you have added to the stress your cat is already feeling.
Instead of stopping the problem, you may have just
accelerated it. Never punish your cat for not using the litter
box. Only use positive methods and reinforcement to solve a
litter box problem.

- Never rub a cat's nose in her accident. Not only is this
  not going to solve the problem, but it will make matters
  worse. In addition, this is completely unhealthy for
  your cat.

Solving the problem of why your cat
does not want to use her litter box
will guarantee a happy home for
you and your cat.

- Never physically place cats into the litter box with
  the idea you are sending the signal to use the box.
  In actuality, this can cause the cat to think she is not
  supposed to use the box and it is a place where she
  gets punished.

- The use of squirt bottles is not recommended. It is difficult
  to use a squirt bottle and not be seen by the cat. If your
  cat sees you, she could become afraid of you.

- Confinement does not necessarily solve the problem long
  term, because you have not addressed why your cat
  quit using the litter box in the first place. Confinement
  may work short term because the confinement area may
  be so small your cat doesn't have a choice but to use
  the box. But long term, we need to solve the problem of
  why your cat quit using his litter box so he can live out
  and about your house as a member of the family.

- Never take an indoor cat and put him outside to live
  because of a litter box problem. Indoor cats are indoor
  cats and should stay that way. You need to work to
  solve the litter box problem for your cat.

- Drugs should be used only as a last resort to correcting
  behavior. Consult a behavior expert and explore all other
  options and modifications before using drug therapy.

Spraying Cats

Determine if the spraying problem is an inside or outside territory issue.

Try the following solutions:

• Feliway® is a synthetic cat pheromone that comes in spray or plug-in form. It is not a drug, so will not cause any long-term harm to your cat. However, it tends to relieve stress in cats and can be useful if the spraying issue is focused inside your home.

• If you discover there are strays or outside cats coming to your house and potentially causing the spraying issue, talk to the owners of the visiting cat. Ask them to keep their cat inside.

• If the cat is a stray, work with the local animal control unit or shelter about humanely live-trapping the stray and getting her to a shelter for care or consider a Trap-Neuter-Return (TNR) Program. See chapter 16.

• Close curtains or blinds so your cat cannot see the outside cat.

• Use outside environmental deterrents, such as determining the time of day the cat may be wandering to your yard and setting up a lawn sprinkler. See Chapter 16.

Dealing with Spraying

Spraying is a separate issue from litter box issues. Spraying is usually, but not always, about territory issues.

When cats "spray," they do it in a horizontal or vertical position. Horizontal means they tend to squat as if they were urinating normally, only they do it outside the box. It is easy to mistake spraying horizontally with regular urination outside the box. You must make sure you are describing it correctly, because the modification is quite different for a spraying cat and one that is not using his litter box.

Vertical means the cat backs up to a wall and sprays the urine on the wall. Vertical spraying needs to be addressed from a behavior standpoint.

Feliway® and other non-drug calming products may be helpful when your cat is stressed and spraying inside your home.

Dealing with Spraying *Continued*

We see an increase in cat behavior calls relating to spraying during the spring and summer months. This makes sense since people tend to let their cats out to roam the neighborhood when the weather is nice. Your indoor cat sees these trespassers on his property and sprays.

To address spraying issues, you must first find out if it is an inside or outside territory issue. Is there a stray cat outside the house that is causing the issue. Or, are there issues inside the house with a new pet or not enough areas for bathroom duties or food stations?

The first priority is to make sure your cat is spayed or neutered. The majority of spayed or neutered cats will not spray, so if your cat is spraying and has not been altered, take care of that matter right away.

If a stray cat outside is the cause of your indoor cats spraying, close the blinds or use outside deterrents to keep the stray away.

Mewsings
Litter Box

Scary Area

Question: "I caught a stray "feral" cat and her kittens in a live trap. They are in my basement in a big kennel. My two indoor cats, Lucy and Gracie, refuse to use their litter boxes or food bowls in the basement. Lucy and Gracie have both started urinating and defecating outside their box—and upstairs. How can I get Lucy and Gracie back to the basement to use their boxes and to eat?"

Answer: I explained that as far as Lucy and Gracie were concerned, there was a monster in the basement—the monster being the wild cat and her kittens. Until that cat and her kittens aren't in the basement anymore, it is unlikely Lucy and Gracie will be going down there. Their owner needs to put litter boxes upstairs, as well as a feeding station.

While Lucy and Gracie's owner had done a good thing by caring for this mother cat and her kittens, she needed to remember she still had to accommodate her indoor cats. After moving the litter and feeding stations upstairs, Lucy and Gracie were back to using their boxes right away, and eating normally. Lucy and Gracie knew to use the box, but were not willing to go to the scary area to do it.

addressing your kitten's wild play

Topics:

Redirect your kitten's wild play to appropriate toys.

Throw a lightweight ball, or Ping Pong ball, away from your kitten for her to chase.

Managing Rough Play

Rough, play-motivated behaviors are common in active cats under two years of age, as well as in cats that live in one-cat households.

Playing allows your cat the opportunity to practice her survival skills. Rough play occurs when your cat moves from a play-motivated emotional state to a predatory state using her claws, teeth or both when over-stimulated. Even though she may be practicing her survival skills, she needs to learn what is appropriate with humans.

Kittens are curious and like to explore new areas. They also like to investigate all moving objects, people and pets. They may bat, bite and pounce on objects to learn about them. Kittens learn how to soften their bite from their mother and littermates. A kitten that is separated from her family too early may play more wildly than a kitten that has had the benefit of learning the rules from her cat family.

You can create behavior problems in a kitten by using your hands or feet when playing instead of appropriate toys. The kitten is being taught that rough play with people is acceptable. In most cases, you can teach your kitten or young adult cat that rough play is not acceptable behavior.

— CAT FACT —

A kitten weighs just 3 ounces at birth and takes up to 2 weeks before being able to hear well.

Encouraging Appropriate Behavior

If your kitten or cat begins to chew on your toes, redirect her aggressive behavior onto acceptable objects like toys.

Drag a toy along the floor to encourage your kitten to pounce on it instead of you. Try throwing a ball away from your kitten allowing her to chase it. Some kittens will even bring it back to be thrown again. A Ping Pong ball works great because it is lightweight and bounces and rolls for a long time, keeping your kitten entertained. *If you have a dog, be careful, as they tend to crunch Ping Pong balls.*

Always be consistent in redirecting your kitten's rough play. Do not allow her to bite your hand one day and scold her for it the next day. This only confuses the kitten and makes it more difficult to teach her appropriate behavior.

A stuffed toy about the same size as your kitten can make a great playmate. Your kitten can wrestle with it, grab it with both front feet, bite it and kick it with her back feet. This is something your kitten did with her littermates when they were young. This is also one of the ways kittens try to play with human feet and hands, so it is important to provide an alternative play target. Encourage play with a "wrestling toy" by rubbing it against your kitten's belly when she starts to play roughly. As soon as she accepts the toy, move your hand out of the way.

Kittens need a lot of playtime. Set up three or four consistent times during the day to initiate play. Teaching your kitten the playtime rules will help her understand she doesn't have to be the one to initiate play by pouncing on you.

Kittens learn from each other, so if there is room in your family you should consider getting another kitten. They will teach each other how to play appropriately. We recommend at least a double cat household.

Mewsings
Play Biting

Biting Feet

Question: "My 3-1/2 year old cat Buddy bites my feet and then runs away. I have tried to stop his behavior by spraying him with a water bottle and by pushing Buddy away."

Answer: Buddy was obviously "play biting". Spraying and pushing him away will only escalate his behavior. When a cat is playing and someone uses a hand or foot to push the cat away, the cat reads that as the human playing back with him. The hand motion and interaction tells the cat the game is on. Typically, cats will actually escalate their play behavior to match what they perceive to be the level of playing the human is doing with them.

Water bottles, while in the past thought to be a great way to train a cat not to do something, actually have a negative effect. He sees his guardian spraying him with water and becomes fearful because he thinks his owner is going to spray him with unwelcome water.

We want cats to build up their relationships with their humans, so we want to use positives to redirect their behavior, not negatives. After explaining this to Buddy's owner, we discussed a new plan that involved using Ping Pong balls to redirect Buddy's behavior.

After a short period of time, Buddy chased after the ball his owner tossed until the ball became more fun than the feet.

Do Not...

Do not tap, flick, or hit your kitten for rough play. These actions are almost always guaranteed to backfire.

Your kitten could become afraid of you or interpret those flicks as play, which could result in even more rough behavior.

Squirt bottles are also a bad idea, since using them can make your kitten afraid of you.

Picking your kitten up for a "time out" could reinforce her behavior, since she probably likes it when you pick her up.

If your kitten is biting through the skin, confine her to a room and seek help from a behavior specialist.

Discouraging Inappropriate Behavior

Set rules for your kitten's behavior from day one.

If you do not have rules, your kitten will make her own. Every person your cat comes in contact with, including visitors, should know and reinforce these rules. For example, your kitten cannot be expected to understand that it is acceptable to play rough with Dad, but not the baby.

Withdrawing Attention

Limits should be set at a point the whole family can follow. It is difficult for your kitten to adjust play styles if someone teaches rough play, then someone else says it is not allowed. None of these methods will be effective unless you give your kitten acceptable outlets for her energy. Supply her with appropriate toys, plenty of playtime or a kitten playmate.

If your kitten starts to play roughly stop the play. If the distraction and redirection techniques don't seem to be working, withdraw all your attention from her. Do this by walking away and leaving her alone in the room. Do not pick her up and move her to another room; she will view that as a reward. She will eventually understand how far she can go if you are consistent.

Seek Help

If your kitten is biting or scratching through the skin, it is best to seek immediate help from a behavior specialist. Keep your kitten confined to a room so she cannot continue the unwanted behavior until you can get help. Thoroughly clean all bites and scratches and consult your physician, as cat scratches and bites can easily become infected.

Adopting a friend for your cat is always recommended. They can teach each other how to play appropriately.

Mewsings
Rough Play

Nipping Solutions

Question: "My cat Marlene is nine months old. She has started to nip at my hands while she sits on my lap. What can I do to get her to top biting me?"

Answer: In essence, Marlene is playing, even though it seems like aggression. There are three main ways to change this behavior.

The first is to "hiss" at Marlene when she bites. It is important to "hiss" at the exact time the cat is biting you. Marlene's mother would have used hissing to correct Marlene's inappropriate behavior, so it often works for humans to do the same thing. Rarely, the cat will simply look at you and go back to what she was doing. But most times the cat will jump off your lap or move away from you quickly. This is the reaction you want. It tells you the cat has received the message that her behavior was inappropriate. Also, you can substitute toys to redirect her play from you to the toys.

The second suggestion is Ping Pong balls. These are lightweight and bounce. The key is when you see Marlene getting ready to bite in play toss the ball across Marlene's line of sight and she will run after the ball instead of biting.

The third and best suggestion is to get a second cat friend for Marlene. Gender isn't an issue, but try to get a cat between six months and two years, so the play drive matches Marlene's age. As an only cat, Marlene is lonely and wants to play and play hard. The two cats will teach each other what is appropriate and what is too wild.

scratching

Provide your cat with appropriate scratching surfaces.

Perfectly Normal Behavior

Scratching is a perfectly normal and necessary feline behavior.

Although scratching does serve to shorten and condition their claws, the primary reasons cats scratch are to mark their territory and to stretch. Cats may also threaten or play with a swipe of their paws.

For cats that live primarily outdoors, scratching is seldom a problem for the owners. It is usually directed at appropriate objects such as tree trunks or fence posts. Play swatting with other cats seldom leads to injuries, because cats have a fairly thick skin and coat for protection. When play does get a little rough, cats are good at sorting things out between themselves. On occasion, rough play or territorial fighting leads to injuries or abscesses that require veterinary attention.

Cats that live primarily or exclusively indoors may run into trouble with their owners when they begin to scratch furniture, walls and doors, or when they use their claws to climb or hang from the drapes. Claws can also cause injuries to people when the cats are overly playful or don't like a particular type of handling or restraint. With a good understanding of cat behavior and a bit of effort, it is possible to prevent or avoid most clawing problems.

It is impractical and unfair to expect cats to stop scratching entirely.

Cats that spend most of their time indoors will require an area for indoor scratching, climbing and playing.

While it may not be possible to stop a cat from scratching, it is possible to redirect the scratching, climbing and playing to appropriate indoor areas. Building or designing a scratching post, providing a cat tree and other appropriate toys and keeping the cat away from potential problem areas is usually adequate when dealing with most scratching problems.

Trimming Claws

You may be able to lessen some of your cat's potential for destruction by carefully trimming his claws. It is important to have your veterinarian show you how to trim them. If you do it incorrectly and cut the "quick," it will be painful for your cat. While the area will physically heal, it could make your cat fearful of claw trims. Trimming claws is a relatively simple task, if you are trained correctly.

Take your time and start by trimming one paw at a time and build from there. Teach your cat that having his claws trimmed is fun and rewarding by offering him a favorite treat as you trim. Ideally, you should trim your cat's claws every few weeks.

If you have a kitten, start trimming early. Teaching your kitten to sit still during claw trimming will be easier if he grows up thinking this is a normal routine. You can teach an older cat to sit relatively still while having his claws trimmed. Patience and going slowly will help him accept having his claws trimmed.

Other Activities

Provide your cat with other stimulation to keep him occupied throughout the day. For ideas, see Chapter 18 and Chapter 10.

Another way to prevent inappropriate scratching.

Soft Paws® are vinyl caps that glue to your cat's claws. They are available in a kit and are easy to use. The vinyl caps are generally applied to the front paws only, since these claws cause most of the destruction to your home. A kit will last approximately three to six months, depending on your cat. After applying the Soft Paws®, check your cat's claws weekly.

— CAT FACT —

According to the American Veterinary Medical Association, declawing of cats should be considered only after attempts have been made to prevent the cat from using its claws destructively or when its clawing presents a zoonotic risk (pertaining to diseases that can be transmitted from animals to humans) for its owner(s).

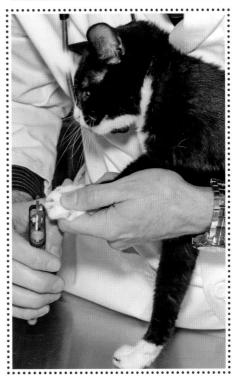

Have your veterinarian show you how to correctly trim your cat's claws.

scratching

Don't Declaw

Declawing is not an acceptable option to stop your cat from scratching. It is literally maiming a cat.

In many countries, declawing is illegal and considered inhumane.

Declawing can lead to physical, emotional and behavioral complications. Some cats can develop an aversion to their litter box because of the pain associated with scratching in the litter after a declawing procedure.

Declawing is not a trivial procedure similar to trimming fingernails. A cat's claws are a vital part of his anatomy, essential to balance, mobility and survival.

Points to Remember

- Don't declaw!
- Understand your cat's need to scratch.
- Provide a suitable place for your cat to scratch.
- Make the scratching post attractive to the cat in height and texture.
- Make the place your cat has been scratching unattractive by using physical or scent-related deterrents.
- Whenever possible, start trimming your cat's claws when he is young.
- Trim your cat's claws, after training by your veterinarian.
- Do not punish—it does not work.

How to Design a Scratching Area

Since cats use their scratching posts for marking and stretching, posts should be set up in prominent areas with at least one post close to the cat's sleeping quarters.

The post should be tall enough for the cat to scratch while standing on his hind legs with the forelegs extended. It should also be sturdy enough so it does not topple when scratched.

Some cats prefer a scratching post with a corner so two sides can be scratched at once. Other cats may prefer a horizontal scratching post. Some scratching posts are even designed to be wall mounted or hung on doors. It is important to observe your cat's scratching behavior and preferences to determine the type of scratching post to get.

Special consideration should be given to the surface texture of the post. Commercial posts are often covered with tightly woven material for durability, but many cats prefer a loosely woven material where the claws can hook and tear the material during scratching.

Scratching is also a marking behavior and cats want to leave a visual mark. Carpet may be an acceptable covering, but it should be combed first to make certain there are no tight loops. Some cats prefer sisal, hessian (a loosely woven fabric like burlap), a piece of fabric from an old chair, or even bare wood for scratching. Be certain to use a material that appeals to your cat.

Getting Your Cat to Use a Post

A good way to get the cat to use the post is to turn the scratching area into an interesting and desirable play center.

Perches to climb on, space to climb into and toys mounted on ropes or springs are all highly appealing to most cats. Placing a few play toys, cardboard boxes, catnip treats or even the food bowl in the area should help to keep the cat interested. Sometimes rubbing the post with tuna oil or catnip will increase its attractiveness. Food rewards can also be given if you observe the cat scratching at his post. Products have been designed to reward the cat automatically by dispensing food rewards each time the cat scratches.

It may be necessary to place the post in the center of a room or near the furniture the cat was trying to scratch until he reliably uses it. You can then move it to a less obtrusive location. For some cats, multiple posts in several locations may be necessary.

Scratching posts with perches and a variety of textures create an interesting play area for your cat. If you have multiple cats you will need multiple scratching areas.

Mewsings

Scratching Furniture

Cat-Proofing Your Home

Question: "What if my cat continues to scratch the furniture?"

Answer: Despite the best of plans and the finest of scratching posts, some cats may continue to scratch or climb in inappropriate areas. At this point a little time, effort and ingenuity might be necessary. Use catnip to sprinkle on the post to draw your cat to it.

If the cat continues to use one or two pieces of furniture, move the furniture or place a scratching post directly in front of it. Cover the furniture with plastic carpet runner with the nubs facing up. Once the cat is using the scratching post instead of your couch, gradually move the post to the spot you would like it to be permanently placed.

Take a good look at the surfaces of the scratched furniture. The surface of the post should be covered with a material similar to the one for which the cat has shown a preference. Placing additional scratching posts in strategic areas may be helpful. Keeping the cat's nails properly trimmed or using Soft Paws® is also helpful for some owners.

Inappropriate Scratching

Indirect, non-physical forms of correcting your cat's behavior may be useful, particularly if you can remain out of sight while administering it.

In this way, the cat may learn that scratching is unpleasant even when you are not present. All forms of physical punishment should be avoided, since it can cause fear or aggression toward you. At best, the cat will learn to stop inappropriate scratching only when you are around.

The best deterrents are those that train the pet not to scratch, even in your absence. If the area can be made less appealing, the cat will likely seek out a new area for scratching - hopefully his scratching post.

An environmental negative is something in the environment which will cause your cat to have a negative association with a particular area, for example, double-sided tape. The benefit of an environmental negative is that it will not affect the relationship you have with your cat, because you were not involved.

Inappropriate Scratching *Continued*

The simplest approach is to cover the surface you don't want your cat to scratch with a less appealing material. Carpet runner plastic turned wrong side up, a loosely draped piece of fabric, aluminum foil or double-sided tape will work.

Another effective deterrent is to booby-trap problem areas so scratching or approaching the area is unpleasant for the cat. Motion detectors or a stack of plastic cups set to topple when the cat scratches will work. You need to be certain any traps you set up will not hurt your cat.

Placing a piece of plastic carpet runner with the nubbed-side out on the arm of a couch will deter your cat from using the couch as a scratching post.

Mewsings
Scratching Furniture

Try a New Post

Question: "My cat Sam scratches my furniture. I am considering declawing him or turning him into an outside cat. The scratching post I have sits on the floor, is covered with carpet and is horizontal in design."

Answer: Sam was scratching the couch in a vertical motion on one of the arms, so I advised his owner to get an upright scratching post covered in sisal and place it close to the spot on the couch Sam was scratching. I also suggested she sprinkle catnip on the post to draw Sam to it. I told her if Sam started using the couch to go over and move him nicely to the post that was nearby.

She called me after night one and indicated that she had done just that—moved Sam the first time he used the couch to the new post and that Sam had immediately started using the post. I told her to make sure the new approach worked multiple times.

After a few days, she called to report that Sam was using the new post and things were working out well.

The key things to note in this case are Sam's owner had to monitor him after the new post came home and redirect him to the new desired place to scratch. Sam was rewarded with "good boy" and food treats a few times to reinforce he was scratching in the appropriate place.

scratching

Cat Scratch Fever

Cat Scratch Fever

There is a disease called cat scratch fever that can be passed to humans.

- It is caused by bacteria called bartonella. This disease is believed to be transmitted by cat scratches, cat bites or exposure to the saliva of an infected cat. Symptoms may occur about two to three weeks after the infection.

- Common human symptoms include a blister at the site of injury (usually the first sign), fatigue, fever, headache, swollen lymph node near the scratch or bite and overall discomfort.

- Generally, cat scratch fever is not serious and medical treatment is not usually needed. In severe cases, treatment with antibiotics can be helpful.

- In children with normal immune systems, full recovery without treatment is the norm. In immune-compromised people, treatment with antibiotics generally leads to recovery.

Cheek Marking

Cats and kittens also mark by rubbing their cheeks on you and secreting scent from glands on their face and head.

Unlike scratching, cheek marking does not leave a visual mark. The scent marking cats and kittens perform is not limited to friends, but extends to inanimate objects, such as furniture and trees. This can define territory or ownership of areas and objects, including you.

Cats will cheek mark furniture and people to define territory and ownership and to show affection.

Mr. Knightly and Max

It was September 2004 and my house was in NEED of a cat since my 17-year-old kitty had died in June. On a busy Saturday morning I visited the main office of the Animal Rescue League to look at the kitties. I wanted a cat that was different from my gray striped tabby. In the back room, I found him—a 16-week-old red-gold male going by the name of Tabby. I knew he was the one when I held him and got no complaints. Because the ARL was so busy, I went back in the afternoon to finalize the paperwork and bring the carrier. "Tabby" settled in immediately and even provided entertainment for a party a few days later by playing the boneless cat. After briefly considering Simba, we landed on the new name of Maximan. He took to a harness without any trouble and amazes many people by walking on his leash. Max is also an extremely smart cat who can get into anything. He can open any door that isn't latched by either pushing or pulling it. Max's little brain goes all the time, and he can become bored, demanding attention and often playing rough. He needed something to keep him occupied during the day.

In August 2008, I stopped by the Ankeny PetSmart and happened to look at the cats available for adoption. In the middle cage was a big, white cat. His name was Wizard. He was declawed, medium length hair, and 5-1/2 years old. I WANTED that cat and couldn't believe someone hadn't already snatched him up. But I already had a cat and didn't really need two, although Max might like some company. It took a couple of days to decide that I really could handle a second cat. Another day passed before I could adopt him, but he was obviously meant to be mine. I called him Mr. Knightly, hoping he would be a good influence on Maximan. I discovered that Mr. Knightly had some health issues. His digestive system was out of whack and he was stressed. His body was bloated and hard, and he threw up daily in addition to having runny and bloody stools. A couple of trips to the vet didn't dramatically improve things. However, he did slowly begin to improve with a consistent diet and stable surroundings. It took at least six months for Mr. Knightly to settle into his new home, much longer than I would have guessed. Maximan and Mr. Knightly have been buddies now for nearly two years. They run, jump and play together and have a system worked out of who gets to sit in the window and who gets the prime spot on the bed. Two successful adoptions!

Amy

Gone to a Good Home!

cat toys and how to use them

Considerations for Choosing Toys

Toys are an important component in keeping your cat emotionally happy.

Choosing the right toys and using them in the right way are equally important. There are literally hundreds of cat toys on the market. It can be difficult to determine which ones are best for your cat and her emotional happiness and growth.

Safety is a factor. The old saying "curiosity killed the cat" can be true. Items that are most curious to cats can be the most dangerous. String, yarn, ribbon, paper clips and rubber bands can all be ingested and cause serious health issues or death for your cat.

Keep your eyes open for dangerous items that may interest your cat. Remove them or move them to an area or container your cat cannot get into. Check labels on stuffed animals. If the item is safe for children under three years old, then the stuffing and parts will likely be safe for your cat. Cats tend to like soft toys they can carry around. Rigid toys aren't attractive and most likely will be ignored.

The age, size and activity level of your cat will play key parts in making decisions about her toys. Cats will have personal preferences as to which toys they favor. Additionally, especially in the days of technology, you need to consider the environment your pet lives in and which toys will be fun, exciting and safe.

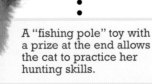

A "fishing pole" toy with a prize at the end allows the cat to practice her hunting skills.

Toys for Active Play

For active cats that really enjoy playing:

Ping Pong balls are a favorite. They are lightweight and bounce and roll easily. Cats love to bat at them, and they are too large to be ingested. Keep in mind, however, some large breed dogs can crack, break and swallow the balls or the fragments. For fun, put several of the balls in a dry bathtub. Show your cat the toys and let them bounce the balls around for hours of enjoyment. Just remember to remove the balls at bedtime or you will hear those Ping Pong balls in the middle of the night.

Sisal-wrapped toys are fun for your cat and depending on the material, she may carry them around the house. Some cats prefer sisal to soft toys.

Empty cardboard rolls from paper towels or toilet paper are fun for many cats. Make them even more fun by unrolling a little of the cardboard to get them started on playtime.

Plastic round shower curtain rings can be batted around as singles or link several together and hang them from a doorknob.

Simple Toys

Find Them at Home

Question: "Are there simple items around the house to use for cat toys? I have two cats and don't want to spend lots of money on toys."

Answer: One of the best toys is a paper sack— not plastic—or a cardboard box. Cats will play with and in these for hours and sometimes even sleep in them. Put them out for play for a couple of days, and then put them out of sight for a week or two. Bring them back out for a fresh set of toys.

Cats love to play in and on paper sacks.

Toys to Avoid

There are some types of toys that should be avoided.

Your fingers and toes should not be used as toys. Such play encourages your cat to think of your hands as toys and this can cause play biting behavior to develop. Additionally, toys that are like gloves or go onto your hands can also cause play biting behavior to develop. Stay away from these types of toys to avoid having problems later.

Catnip can become an issue for some cats. Some cats play with catnip toys or eat catnip, and they can relax and have fun. For others, however, catnip can affect personality in a negative way. They get over-stimulated, which can increase play biting or other undesirable behaviors.

Toys for Active Play *Continued*

"Fishing poles" are great toys for you to use when playing with your cat. You can sit and watch television and play with your cat at the same time. You should always be sure to let your cat "catch" the prize at the end of the pole, so she feels her hunting is working. Play with your cat, let her catch it, and then play some more. This will keep your cat from becoming bored and frustrated. Plus, it makes her feel good.

Toys for Comfort

Try these toys for cats that want comfort, but not necessarily play:

Cardboard boxes can be a comfort toy. If using a box for comfort vs. active play, make sure the box is big enough for your cat to get in and lie down. Cats also use cardboard boxes for active play—jumping in, lying and hiding inside.

Cardboard boxes can be used for active play or comfort.

Toys for Comfort *Continued*

Stuffed animals are a favorite. Provide ones that are small enough to carry around or lie on. If you have a cat that wants to hunt the toy and "kill it," make sure the stuffed animal is about the size of your cat. Toys that have parts such as legs or tails are even more fun and attractive for play.

Provide your cat with stuffed toys she can carry around or lie on.

Getting the Most from Toys

Provide your cat with toys, use the toys and allow your cat to have fun with them. These suggestions may help you do that:

Rotate your cat's toys weekly, making only a few toys available at a time. Keep a variety of toys out and easily accessible. If your cat has a favorite toy, such as a stuffed mouse or soft toy for cuddling, leave it out all the time. You don't want to rotate the comfort toys, just the play toys.

Provide several toys—one that allows your cat to "hunt," one to baby, one to carry around and one to play and bat around. Rotate toys so your cat has at least one of these out at all times.

Caution on laser lights. Use them sparingly, as a lot of cats become over-stimulated by the rapid movement. When this happens, even when you stop, the cat will keep looking with obsession, which is not good for her emotionally.

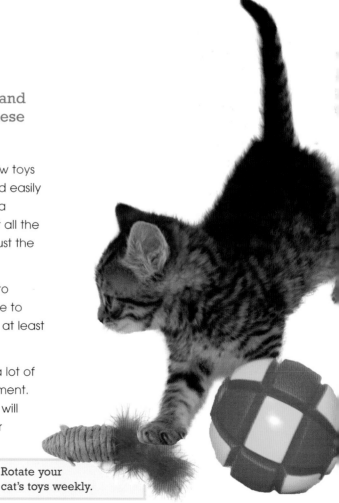

Rotate your cat's toys weekly.

everyone needs more than a cat nap

Topics:

Why Is My Cat Keeping Me Awake?

"My cat is keeping me awake at night" is a common complaint among pet owners.

However, if you think about it, it makes sense. Cats are nocturnal, so it is normal for them to be awake and active at night. However, this can be a problem for you when you are trying to sleep and they want to play. Punishing your cat is never acceptable, especially when she is demonstrating her natural behavior.

The first question we ask is, "What do you do when your cat wants your attention at night?" The answer is almost always, "I get up and play with her for a while" or "I get up and feed her." These responses to your cat's behavior will not get you a good night's sleep. By getting up to play or give her food you are reinforcing your cat's behavior. She is getting what she wants which results in her repeating the behavior night after night. Even if you push your cat away or tell her "No!" you are still responding and giving her attention. You need to completely ignore your cat until the behavior stops. You must also provide toys and playtime with you before going to bed.

If your cat is bored and sleeps all day, chances are she will be keeping you awake all night.

> — **CAT FACT** —
> Cats sleep approximately two-thirds of the day. This translates into 16 hours of sleeping and 8 hours of being active.

Change Your Cat's Routine

You have two options when your cat is active at night.

Switch her sleep schedule so she is sleeping at night and active during the day or give her things to occupy her at night so you can sleep. Switching your cat's sleep schedule can be difficult if you are not home during the day to tire her out by keeping her awake or playing with her.

You can try computer software or a DVD that has optical appeal to a cat, such as one with fish or birds moving across the screen. Watching this will keep your cat alert and interested in something other than sleep during the day. This is also a good nighttime device.

Place bird feeders outside your cat's favorite window. The birds will give your cat something other than a nap to focus on during the day.

At night, provide activities and new things to keep your cat occupied while you are sleeping. Switch out toys every few days so she doesn't become bored. Play with her when you get home at night and throughout the evening. This doesn't have to be solid hours of play. Ten minutes of running after a Ping Pong ball or jumping for a fishing pole toy will seem like a long time to your cat. See chapter 10 for more information on appropriate and safe cat toys.

Be consistent and don't give up. It may take a few days or even a few weeks, but it will be worth the effort.

> **TIP:** Never allow your cat to use your bed or bedroom as a play area. This will help them understand it is off-limits at night for playtime.

Mewsings
Sleeping Arrangements

Shut the Door!

Question: "My cat, Gus, is keeping me awake at night. I have tried shutting him out of my bedroom, but he bangs on the door and I still can't sleep."

Answer: I suggested she put pillows in front of the door (on the outside) making it impossible for Gus to hit the door. His owner called a week later and said it had worked. Eventually she didn't even have to use the pillows because Gus had gotten the message that once the door was closed, she wasn't getting up to let him in.

Mewsings
Hair Chewing

Cats Like Hair

Question: "My cat, Wally, is chewing on my hair while I am sleeping. How can I get him to stop?"

Answer: I explained to her that some cats like the "taste" or feel of hair in their mouth. Wally's owner had been pushing him away and telling him "no!" but those deterrents weren't working. He kept coming back every night for more hair chewing. I explained to her that by pushing him away she was still giving Wally attention. Instead we needed to come up with a deterrent that was 'natural' so her hair wouldn't be fun to chew on anymore. I suggested a hair net for a few nights, or to put a bad-tasting hair spray on before she went to bed. Wally would then start to chew as normal and discover he didn't like the smell or taste of the hairspray or the feel of the hair net, and the behavior would stop.

Adopt a Friend

Getting your cat a friend can be the solution to your night play or disruption problem. Time and time again it has solved the problem. The two nocturnal cats play and keep each other company while you sleep. A second cat is also great company for your cat during the day when you are gone. Visit your local animal shelter, adopt a cat and everyone wins.

Adopt a playmate for your cat. They will entertain each other during the day and at night.

Some happy endings
from the Animal Rescue League of Iowa

McGee

McGee is a four-year-old buff tabby. He was known as Cornelius at the ARL South location. I just adopted him July 28, 2011, and he's already settled in brilliantly.

Not much is known about his history prior to coming to the ARL, except that he was a stray. I came into the South location not even really having my heart set on taking a cat home that day. I'd been thinking about it and doing research, so I figured, "What's the harm in looking?"

McGee laid eyes on me and never let go. He came right to me, settled into my lap, headbutted me, and purred the entire time. He essentially chose me. Honestly, what can you do when that happens?

In the short time I have had him, McGee has provided an endless supply of affection and love. He's a HUGE cuddle monster and loves sleeping in my bed right next to me. He's not very interested in toys, but loves his mealtimes and to be petted. He has some spats with the other two cats that belong to my roommate, but nothing serious.

He prefers human company anyway.

Katie

Bella

We adopted Bella in June 2010 from the ARL Main location. We were told that she was surrendered by the roommate of her former owner, after the owner moved out and abandoned her. We get some skeptical looks when we tell the story of how Bella chose us, but it is absolutely true. While we had her in the visiting room at ARL, the volunteer came back to see how we were doing. I said that I really liked her, but my husband wasn't completely sold. She was friendly and sweet, but so quiet and he said he likes a cat that will talk to you. Right then she let out a quiet little meow. We looked at each other, then down at her in disbelief and she meowed again! And that was when we knew it was meant to be.

These days Bella is living the life. She made good friends with our existing cat, and they really enjoy playing together. Bella spends a lot of time monitoring the bird activity from her perch on the windowsill. She plays fetch the hair tie with my husband (yes, she brings it back!). She loves to jump on my shoulder, rub her face against my cheek while purring, and ride around. She fits right into our family and we are so grateful to the ARL for bringing us together.

Gina

the fearful cat

Topics:

Manageable Fears

Behaviors to Check Out

When to Have a Behavioral Consultation

A Plan of Action

Manageable Fears

Balloons, plastic sacks and loud noises are common fears among cats. These fears are manageable.

There are many reasons cats develop fears.

Socialization - They may have had limited exposure to other animals and people when they were young. Socialization is an important aspect of raising a kitten. The socialization window for kittens starts to close at twelve weeks of age. Without adequate, continuous and positive interaction with people and other animals, cats may develop fears.

Negative experience - Cats can learn fear from just one negative, traumatic experience. You may not have thought it was a big deal, but it might have been from the cat's perspective. This experience may stick with the cat in future similar situations. For example, a bad experience with a small child could result in a cat that is fearful of all small children.

A number of unpleasant events associated with a person or animal can sometimes lead to increasing fear. For example, if a pet is punished or some disturbing event occurs in the presence of a particular person or other animal, he may begin to associate that person or other animal with the unpleasant consequence or punishment.

Genetics is another important contributing factor to the development of fear. There are some cats that are inherently timid and fearful. These animals may never become outgoing and social.

All these fears are manageable. Shelter cats have no more fears than a cat you might find as a stray or get from a pet shop, breeder, friend or the Internet. Adopting a cat is always the way to go.

When your cat is afraid she may try to hide. Do not force her out of hiding as this will add to her fear.

Behaviors to Check Out

When your cat is frightened, he may try to appear smaller, place his ears back, be immobile and want to hide.

In addition, he may show signs of agitation or aggression, such as dilated pupils, arched back, piloerection (hair standing on end), hissing or growling.

Before you seek any behavioral help, see your veterinarian and get a complete medical examination for your pet, including blood work. This will determine if there is a medical condition contributing to the behavior problem.

When to Have a Behavioral Consultation

A behavioral consultation with your veterinarian, veterinary behaviorist or animal behavior specialist is needed for cats showing extreme fears or aggression.

If the fears are mild, owner intervention may help prevent them from progressing. Begin by identifying the fear-causing problem. This is not always easy and needs to be exact. You will need to determine which person or animal makes the cat afraid, as well as where the fearful behavior occurs. Often there are certain situations, people and places that provoke the behavior more than others.

For treatment to be successful, it is important to identify and work around the situations, people, places and animals least likely, as well as most likely, to cause the fear.

Before a behavior modification program can begin, you must be able to control your cat. This can be accomplished with a figure-eight harness and leash, or, if needed, a cage. Next, teach your cat to pair the fearful situation with food rewards. The goal of this training is to allow the cat to assume a relaxed and happy body posture and facial expression in the presence of the problem that used to cause the fear.

Dilated pupils, an arched back and signs of agitation all indicate a fearful cat.

Your Reaction

Owner responses such as anxiety, fear, a raised voice or any form of punishment will only increase your pet's fear or anxiety.

Similarly, a fear- or anxiety-inducing stimulus presented to your cat will further aggravate her anxiety.

Be sure to retrain with calm control.

The goal of training is to reinforce appropriate, desirable responses. Therefore, it is critical that rewards are not given while the cat is displaying an inappropriate response. Of course, if there is any chance of injury, then quickly and safely removing the cat from the situation will have to take priority.

A Plan of Action

A program of counter-conditioning and desensitization is useful for training your cat to handle situations he finds fearful.

Simply put, your cat should be exposed to the fearful stimulus in a slow and compassionate manner until he sees there is nothing to fear and settles down. If the association with the fear-factor can be turned into one that is positive, your cat should gradually develop a positive attitude when exposed to it again.

How to Desensitize

Desensitization is a process of gradual exposure to a fearful stimulus. That sounds fancy, but putting it simply, it involves getting used to the fearful stimulus or situation little by little.

Desensitization involves controlled exposure to situations or stimuli that might cause fear at levels that are minimal enough your cat can still take treats or play games. Therefore, he associates the fearful stimulus with having fun. If at any stage your cat stops taking the treats or stops playing, it means the fearful stimulus is too close and you have gone too far too soon. Allow the cat to leave the area if he so desires.

In combination with counter-conditioning, desensitization is designed to change a pet's attitude or feeling about the stimulus from one that is negative to one that is positive. It involves controlled exposure to situations that might cause fear at levels that are minimal enough that your cat will adapt.

Do not reward your cat with treats or play when she is giving an inappropriate response. Remember not to force your cat during the retraining process or her fearfulness will increase.

A Plan of Action *Continued*

Counter-Conditioning

Counter-conditioning is then used to change the cat's response to a person, animal or situation in a gradual but progressive way. This is done by training the cat to perform or display an acceptable response, such as play or food acquisition, each time he is exposed to the thing he fears. Rather than attempting to overcome his fear all at once, the training should be set up to expose the cat to the fearful subjects at level of reduced intensity to ensure a successful outcome.

Desirable responses should be encouraged and rewarded, so the cat develops a new more desirable behavior in response to the fearful person, animal or situation. Training should never be pushed to the point where the cat feels the need to escape. If the cat's attention can be successfully diverted, the appropriate response can then be rewarded.

Mewsings
Fearful Cat

The disappearing cat

Question: "What can I do about my cat Tess? She is afraid of kids and whenever my grandkids come over, she disappears somewhere in the house. I can't even find her."

Answer: Cats that are afraid and take themselves out of a situation should be left alone. People make a big mistake by pulling the cat out of her hiding place and taking her to the kids to show there is nothing to fear. The cat is already afraid and should be left to keep herself out of a situation.

In situations where the cat doesn't completely disappear, you can help to ease her fear. When the kids appear to stress out the cat, be sure they have treats in their hands. Have the kids put the treats down in front of the cat, or as close as they can get without her running off. Have the kids walk away. This shows the cat that when the kids come to the house, good things happen. In this case, the good things are the treats.

You can also use a toy, such as a cat fishing pole if the cat loves to play. Have the kids wave the fishing pole in a slow manner beside the cat. Hopefully, the cat starts to play and it reinforces that when the kids come to the house, good things (play in this example) happen.

Never force the cat to interact with the kids if it causes stress. Let the cat hide if she wants and come out when she is ready.

who says your cat can't talk to you?

Topic:

Cat Communication

Cat Communication

Cats do communicate with their owners.

How they communicate and the frequency depends on the cat.

Some cats never make a sound, while others meow, chirp and vocalize on a regular basis. When you work around multiple cats at an animal shelter or live with more than one cat, the differences in a cat's vocalization pattern are clearly noticeable.

Cats make sounds for different reasons, from trying to get your attention at dinnertime to not feeling well physically or emotionally. Even specific cat breeds tend to vocalize more. The underlying reasons as to why a cat meows, yowls or chirps are all different; but in every case it is a communication to their humans or other animals in the household.

One of the best ways to illustrate these talkative cats is to use my own as an example. I live with seven cats, all of which talk or vocalize for different reasons.

— **CAT FACT** —

A cat can make over 100 different sounds.

Cats communicate with their humans and housemates in many ways including vocalization.

Cat Communication *Continued*

Non-talkative

Oscar is a domestic medium hair cat that I have had for over three years. He has not made a sound as long as I have had him. He purrs when I pet him or when he lays beside me, but otherwise as the saying goes, he is quiet as a church mouse.

Breed

Gracie is a Siamese that was abandoned on my porch when she was six weeks old. She meows 'hello' every time she sees me and when she wants attention. When I began researching, I found out quickly the Siamese breed is known for being talkative.

When people ask me what breed of cat to adopt, I tell them to be sure and recognize that some cats are known to be more talkative than others. This can be an issue when you are trying to sleep or have quiet time. Different cat breeds have different characteristics.

Mealtime

Stitch is a domestic shorthair cat who meows like the world is ending if his food bowl is nearly empty. He came to me as a stray and was starving, so food is important to Stitch. He meows 'hello' every now and again, but a nearly empty food bowl gets Stitch meowing and howling until the bowl is filled.

Medical

Beso is a Havana Brown cat. He is relatively quiet, except when he is sick. When he is not feeling well, he meows often, very quietly to make sure I know he is not feeling well.

Jack is a domestic shorthair. Since he turned 17 he has started yowling sporadically. After a few visits to the vet to make sure he wasn't sick, it was determined that old age was causing Jack to make this horrible yowling noise. When he begins to yowl I just pet him until he quiets down.

OSCAR

GRACIE

STITCH

BESO

JACK

Cat Communication *Continued*

Warning

BELLA

Bella is a calico cat that never meows. However, she does growl quite loudly when she sees Gracie, her cat housemate. They are not fans of each other and Bella will instantly start growling when she sees her. This is a communication warning to Gracie to get away. Unfortunately, Gracie rarely listens.

Talkative

OCHO

Ocho is a domestic shorthair cat that is completely deaf. He talks more than any other cat I have and uses different vocals and ranges depending on his message. For example, when he sees I am home he meows a simple 'hello'. If he gets locked out of the bedroom at night he will meow loudly for as long as it takes to get me to open the door for him to come in. When I do open the door (and I know I shouldn't if I want him to stop!) he comes in and changes to a scolding tone for leaving him out. Then he will come and lay by me and start to softly meow and purr to let me know all is forgiven.

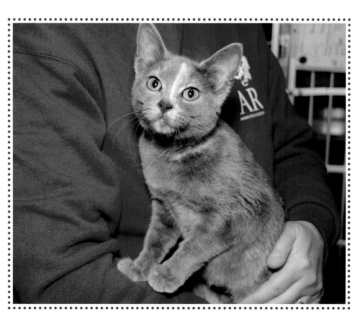
Some breeds of cats 'talk' more than others.

Grief

It has been reiterated to me over the years that a cat's meow can be caused by grief. The loss of another cat or dog friend or settling into a new home and feeling insecure can be a source of grief. The best thing to do is keep your cat to her schedule and pet and talk to her in a calm and soothing voice. The meowing will decrease and eventually cease. Remember, in most cases scolding a cat to 'be quiet!' will do nothing. The very fact you are talking to them will keep them talking to you, no matter what tone you are using.

Attention Seeking

We receive a handful of calls or emails every year from pet owners whose cat's meowing is 'driving them crazy'. Depending on the reason for the meowing, one of the most consistent things you can do is not react. If your cat meows to get you to pet her and you do, she is going to keep meowing because it has worked in the past. Instead, get up and walk away or completely ignore her. When your cat is quiet, pet her. This reinforces that meowing gets her nothing. Quiet gets her what she wants.

Whatever the reason for your cat's meow or other vocalization, it is important as a loving owner to try to understand. Then, when something is wrong, you will hear what your pet is trying to tell you.

Some happy endings
from the Animal Rescue League of Iowa

Charlie

We had recently adopted a younger cat and noticed that our older cats were not interested in playing with her. After talking to the ARL cat behaviorist we decided to adopt a cat closer to her age to be her buddy. I went to the ARL website to look at adoptable cats that were close to her age, and then choose four for my husband and me to meet. We fell in love with all four cats, but decided to adopt Charlie since he had been waiting the longest for a home. He is a big brown tabby with tons of personality. He acclimated to our home with ease. Charlie enjoys belly rubs, sitting on the screened porch and he loves food. We have to hide the cat treats in the freezer because he learned how to open the cupboards and was serving treats at all hours of the day and night! Just thinking about Charlie makes me smile. He is curious, smart and he loves to play—he is a great addition to our family and I love him.

Lora

natural aversives for cats

Topics:

Defining the term

● **Aversive:** defined as causing avoidance of a thing, situation or behavior by using an unpleasant stimulus.

Aversives can be used to turn back, repel or deter the behavior of your cat without harming him.

In no way should aversives be harmful or create fear in your cat.

When using environmental aversives or things that are natural aversives for cats, you need to remember one of the challenges to modifying behaviors in cats is that you may have to do a little trial and error. What works as a natural aversive with one cat may not work with all cats. Just as with humans, individual preferences will vary with each cat. Aversives are often the best method to discourage a cat from a particular action, but will seldom work effectively without offering a rewarding alternative. For example, if you place double-sided carpet tape on your counter, when the cat jumps on it he will have an unpleasant sensation. His reward for staying off the counter is not experiencing that unpleasantness.

Textures and Odors

Use unpleasant textures and smells to keep your cat off counters and furniture indoors. You may also use them on any outdoor areas you want to keep him away from. Remember, these items are meant to deter, not harm.

> **TIP:** If you plan to use textures to deter your cat from counter tops or furniture, weighting the textured material down or taping it may be necessary for it to stay in place.

Protect your furniture or floor finish from sticky substances by securing it to plastic and using canned goods or other weights to hold the plastic in place. Be sure that whatever you use is safe for your cat and will not fall on or hurt your cat.

Use natural aversives to keep your cat off furniture and countertops.

Textures

Indoor

Countertop - Place shelf paper, sticky side up, on the countertop when it is not in use. It will only take one or two sticky landings for your cat to decide the counter is no longer fun. You can also use double-sided carpet tape in the same way.

Furniture - Wrapping chair or table legs with heavy aluminum foil or plastic will deter your cat from scratching the furniture. Scratching is a natural behavior so be sure to give her a scratching alternative, such as a scratching post. See chapter 9.

Outdoor

Flower beds – Irregular-shaped or sharp rocks and pinecones, firmly set into the dirt are uncomfortable for your cat's paws. Make sure the rocks will not cut your cat's skin. This also works with indoor houseplants.

Garden - Chicken wire, set firmly into dirt with the sharp edges rolled under, will keep your cat from digging in the vegetable garden.

Indoors or Outdoors

Plastic carpet runner works well inside or outside and is an inexpensive deterrent to a counter-jumping cat. Turn the carpet runner over so the pointy side is up. This is not painful for your cat, but it is uncomfortable under paws and will make your cat think twice before jumping on the counter or outside deck table.

A plastic carpet runner, with the nub side up, makes an unpleasant landing spot for a cat that likes to jump on the counter.

The same plastic runner can be used on furniture to prevent your cat from scratching.

Irregular-shaped rocks set into the dirt will discourage your cat from digging in your flower bed.

natural aversives for cats

Odor

It may take some trial and error to determine which odors your cat finds offensive. Each cat will react differently to different smells. Remember to always check for toxicity. If the product is safe for young children, it is generally safe for pets, but always check to be certain.

Household items – Insect repellent, colognes, muscle rubs and aloe gel are possible deterrents.

Specialty items – Pet-safe products, available in pet stores, are designed specifically to deter your cat.

Grocery items – Orange or other citrus peels and concentrated juices generally work well.

Begin by protecting your carpets, upholstery, floors or furniture from surface damage by placing weighted foil or heavy plastic at the spot you want your cat to avoid. Soak cotton balls or rags in the "smelly" substance. If using odors as a deterrent outside you may want to place the rags on heavy plastic as the substance may soak into the ground. Outside the odor will lose its potency quickly and will need to be reapplied daily.

Taste

Using taste as a deterrent can be very effective but there are a few things to consider.

- Make sure any taste deterrent you choose is safe for people and pets.

- Some substances may damage furniture or floor finishes. Test them in a hidden location before wide-spread use.

- Taste deterrents developed for pets, like Bitter Apple or similar sprays and gels, are marketed specifically for taste aversion. Always read the instructions carefully before using.

- Insect repellents, especially those containing citronella or citrus odors, are an effective taste and odor aversive. Remember to check for toxicity.

> **Tip:** From experience orange and citrus odors work well, since most cats don't like the smell naturally.

Citrus or orange odors are a natural deterrent for most cats. Check for toxicity and protect wooden surfaces with plastic.

Noises that Startle

Items that deliver a "surprise" value to startle your cat and deter it from going into an area or jumping on the countertop are available commercially or you can create your own. These devices are meant to startle your cat, not hurt her. The information provided is to help you make an informed decision prior to use.

WARNING: Do not use startling aversives on fearful or anxious cats without first consulting with a feline behavior specialist.

Remote

- Use an aluminum pie plate and put water, beans or pebbles in it. Balance it precariously on a counter or other undesirable "jumping" surface. When your cat jumps on the counter, the pie plate will fall making a loud, startling noise. After a few of these "surprise" experiences your cat won't find the counter very appealing.

- Motion detectors that make a startling sound or deliver a shot of air can also be purchased.

Human

It is important your cat does not see you using the items listed to get their attention.

- A loud air horn, whistle or "shaker can" (a soda can filled with pennies, beans or pebbles and taped securely shut) can be used to get your cat's attention and interrupt her unwanted behavior. Always be ready to give your cat an alternate activity.

If your cat sees you using the air horn or blowing the whistle and making the noise they hate, he will start to be afraid of you and not the items. You do not want to jeopardize your relationship with your cat by using these techniques. **If you can't set up these aversives without being seen, do not use these techniques.**

Some happy endings
from the Animal Rescue League of Iowa

Lexi

We already had four cats so when my husband came up to me at the ARL Pet-A-Porter fashion show and told me he saw a kitten he wanted to adopt I was a bit surprised. Being the animal lover that I am, I quickly said show me which one. Next thing I knew we were adopting an adorable six-month-old Scottish Fold, soon to be named Lexi. I like to joke and say "my husband sure knows how to pick them" as Lexi is a wonderful cat, very affectionate and playful. We are very happy to have her as a part of our family and she seems to feel the same way.

Lora

Gone to a Good Home!

Chapter 15

keeping your cat safe - inside and out

Topics:

Inside

Outside

There is a long running debate on whether cats should live indoors, outdoors or a combination of both.

The simple fact is inside cats live much longer than outside cats. The dangers to your cat that exist outdoors do not exist inside the house.

Can a cat that has lived outside live happily indoors? The Animal Rescue League takes in thousands of 'outside strays' every year. The ARL adopts these cats out with the idea that they will be inside house cats. The ease by which outdoor cats can be confined to their homes without any problems makes me believe cats can easily live indoors as part of the family. There is no reason to let your cat outside to annoy neighbors or risk her safety.

Inside

Your cat can live indoors happily. The wanting-to-go-outside feeling your cat has will cease if you make the inside a fun and comforting place for her. Take these steps to make the inside as desirable as the outside.

Provide your cat with a fun and comfortable indoor environment, such as areas for your cat to sun herself.

- Set up bird feeders outside your cat's favorite window so she gets the mental stimulation of the outdoors.

- Grow some cat grass in an inside planter so she can still 'eat' grass.

- Make sure there are sunny spots where your cat can lay.

- Have lots of different cat toys for her to play with inside the house.

- Adopt another cat so she has a cat friend.

- Open windows where your cat cannot escape but will allow the smell of the outdoors to come in.

Once your cat has everything she really needs indoors, she will stop going to the door to be let out after a few weeks.

Outside

Despite the saying that cats have nine lives, they really don't. They do not know to stay out of the street, how to avoid being hit by a car, and as much as we would like, we really can't teach our cats to stay in the yard. If you feel you must allow your cat outside time, follow these suggestions to help keep her as safe as possible.

In the yard - Use a cat collar and correctly fitted harness. You should always supervise your cat while on a harness so she doesn't get entangled or injured on a fence or other outside hazard. The collar and harness is a way to let your cat be outside with you, but safely secure in the yard.

On the deck - Do not put your cat on a collar and tether on an off-ground deck. If she can reach the edge, she could accidentally step over the edge and hang herself. This is another reason your cat should always be supervised outdoors.

Fenced-in yards - Do not assume a fence will contain your cat. Even cats that have been declawed may still be able to scale a six-foot wood fence and take off for the neighbor's house.

Remember, just because you used to let your cat outside, it doesn't mean you should continue to do so. Start keeping her inside. With patience and a short period of adjustment, your cat will live happily and safely in the house with you.

> Neutering or spaying your cat will help reduce the amount of crying or yowling at the door. Cats will typically emit this behavior when they have a need to mate.

Always supervise your cat when she is outdoors. If you have an off-ground deck do not put a tether on your cat if she can reach the edge. It is a choking and hanging hazard.

— CAT FACTS —

- The average life-expectancy of an indoor cat is 16 years or longer.

- A cat who lives outside, lives an average of 3-5 years.

dealing with free-roaming cats

Look around any animal shelter and you will see "stray" listed as the reason many cats are there. These are often free-roaming cats that a kind human found and took to the shelter for care, and hopefully adoption.

Types of Free-Roaming Cats

Domesticated - You may find it surprising that many free-roaming cats are actually very domesticated and sweet – even those you have to humanely live trap because they initially won't let you get close to them.

Feral - Other cats that are humanely trapped may be domestic cats that have returned to a semi-wild state, never kept as pets or feral in nature. These cats are very difficult for an animal shelter to place into a home. They can, however, be part of a cat colony that is spayed or neutered and returned to the same area as long as there is a caretaker to ensure food, water, shelter and medical attention when necessary

Problems

Outdoor, or free-roaming cats can cause problems for you and your neighbors.

- Using yards, gardens or sandboxes as a litter box
- Getting into garages or other buildings
- Chasing away birds from feeders
- Walking on cars and leaving paw prints
- Getting into garbage cans

Solutions

The animal shelter often gets calls asking us how to deal with free-roaming cats. People don't want to hurt the cats and don't blame them for looking for food or using something as a litter box, but they want the cats to leave their yards, cars, birds and property alone.

Free-roaming cats, whether domesticated or feral, can cause some issues for you and your neighbors, but outside free-roaming cats should always be treated humanely.

Dealing with Free-Roaming Cats *Continued*

As with all of our behavior recommendations, we want to deal with these issues using positive reinforcement or humane methods.

- **Determine if the cat is a stray or someone's pet.** If the cat is owned and you know where it belongs, ask the owner to keep the cat inside. If there is no owner, then the cat needs to be taken somewhere safe, such as an animal shelter. She can be inside and properly cared for, as well as spayed or neutered so she isn't reproducing in an already cat over-populated world. Of course, the ideal solution is for all cat owners to keep their cats safely indoors.

- **Use natural deterrents such as odor, texture and movement.** Yelling out your door to get the cat out of the garden is not going to work. The cat will be afraid of you and not understand you simply want her out of your garden. She will only learn not to visit when you are around.

    Odor - Cats, in general, dislike the smell of citrus. Place oranges or orange scent around the area you want the cat to stay away from. The cat will associate the garden or other area with the citrus smell and move on.

    Texture - Plastic carpet runners turned upside down on the hood of your car will create an uncomfortable resting place for a cat. Keep it there for a few weeks. The cat will decide the hood of your car is not a good bed or sunning spot and she will move on. The plastic carpet runner, pointed side up, can also be used around your garden to make an unpleasant walking and digging surface.

    Movement - Motion detector sprinkler systems in the garden are a very effective deterrent. The cat will be startled and a little wet, but will remain unharmed.

- **Hang bird feeders up high or in areas a cat cannot reach.** Do not put feeders on your deck railing or on the ground. Bird feeders need to be in places a cat can't reach. Products are available to keep squirrels from climbing up to bird feeders. These products will also deter cats.

— CAT FACTS —
Overpopulation

- The average number of litters a fertile cat produces is one to two a year; average number of kittens is 4-6 per litter.

- It is impossible to determine how many stray dogs and cats live in the United States; estimates for cats alone range up to 70 million.

- In approximately seven years, an un-spayed female cat and one un-neutered male cat and their offspring can result in over 400,000 kittens.

Birds can be protected from free-roaming cats with products developed to deter squirrels.

dealing with free-roaming cats

Cats are naturally curious. Keep garage doors closed and lids on garbage cans.

- **Keep lids on garbage cans and garage doors closed.** Cats are extremely curious. Exploring buildings and sifting through garbage cans is a natural instinct for them.

- **There are commercial products on the market to repel cats.** These products have been deemed safe by the EPA. Check with your local pet or garden store for more information on these products.

- **Never put out or use poison.** Not only is it inhumane and unnecessary, but you could poison other animals or even children by mistake. Plus, it will only take care of one cat and not keep other cats away.

— **CAT FACT** —

According to the National Council on Pet Population Study and Policy (NCPPSP), less than 2 percent of cats are returned to their owners. Most of these were identified with tags, tattoos or microchips.

(Source: NCPPSP)

Odor, texture and movement are natural deterrents you can use to keep cats off your property. These deterrents are not meant to harm the roaming cat.

Humanely Trapping a Free-Roaming Cat

How do you catch a free-roaming cat?

Option 1: See if the cat is friendly enough to let you pick her up. Offer the cat some food and see if she will come to you to get it. If so, it is a good sign that you will at some point be able to earn the cat's trust and she will let you pick her up. Have a cat carrier handy so when you are able to pick the cat up you can put her into the carrier immediately. Be patient, the process can be slow and methodical and require some time.

Option 2: A humane trap is a device you can buy at a hardware or pet supply store. Animal control agencies often loan or will rent these types of traps. The trap should have food and water set up in it. Ideally, the cat will enter the trap to get food and trigger the door to close leaving the cat inside.

If you choose to use a trap, make sure you are available to check it every few hours so the cat is not without water or in harsh weather for more than an hour. Never trap a cat and take her to an area down the road or out in the country and let her go. Leave the cat in the trap and take her to an animal shelter or contact a local TNR Program. See page 109.

Humane traps are available for sale at hardware or pet stores, or may be available for loan from your local animal control agency.

Outside safety issues

Question: "Two cats were dumped at my house in the country. I have been trying to get closer to them by softly meowing and offering food. I have been doing this for a few weeks but to no avail. I am starting to worry about the cats' safety, due to their being outside all this time."

Answer: We decided to try humanely live trapping and she was able to catch them both within two days. She took the cats to the ARL and after getting them out of the traps, we found both of them to be very sweet and loving. Both were placed for adoption after the appropriate hold time. They were adopted into homes. Follow-up showed both cats were sweet, loving inside cat family members and using their litter boxes.

Some happy endings
from the Animal Rescue League of Iowa

Sweetie Pie

My husband and I adopted Sweetie Pie in October 2008. Since I volunteer with the cats I had been keeping an eye out for a special guy. I tell everyone that Sweetie chose me. The first time I petted him, he turned belly up and licked my nose. I knew then that he was the one!

Since he was found as a stray we didn't know much about Sweetie's history. We could tell he had always been an outdoor cat so we weren't sure how well he would adjust to being cooped up in our apartment. As it turns out he prefers it! He appreciates being safe from the elements.

Sweetie likes his new life as king of the great indoors. I have to watch where I step because he will sleep sprawled out, belly up, with a big cat grin on his face. He has learned to enjoy, even demand, laps. He will wrap his front paws around my leg, rest his chin on my knee and heave a sigh of pure contentment. Then he falls asleep and so do my legs because he weighs over 16 pounds! But we love him and consider ourselves lucky to have found him. He truly is our Forever Friend.

Deirdre and Chris

Feral Cats

You don't typically see feral cats up for adoption at your local animal shelter.

There is a lot of confusion as to what is a feral cat.

When we get calls from the public asking for help with cat behavior issues, they sometimes say their cat is wild and feral.

When we start to inquire as to where the cat stays and sleeps and if she is good with other pets and kids, we discover the cat just has bad manners or needs a playmate.

Feral cats are described as the offspring of other cats that are not spayed or neutered. They are wild in the sense they are not used to human touch or interaction. Most of the time, they have to be live-trapped to be moved or brought into the shelter, since they won't allow themselves to be caught. They are like wild animals that want to avoid humans.

Feral female cats can become pregnant as early as five months of age and can give birth up to three times in a year. All of these pregnancies, starting at an early age and living on the streets, is stressful on these adult feral cats. Their kittens, if they live on the streets, will be feral as well. More than half of these kittens are likely to die without human intervention.

Males who roam and fight to find mates and defend their territories may be injured and transmit diseases to one another through bite wounds. They may also live in pain because of these wounds.

Feral cats deserve compassion and understanding, and to be cared for as much as the cats that share our homes and lives. Feral cats and their offspring are often victims of abandonment or being born in the wild. The life they know is simply trying to survive on the streets.

Adult feral cats do not typically adapt to living as pets in someone's home. Success is possible with kittens if they are gotten early enough. They need to be constantly handled and socialized, and they must be introduced to socialization almost immediately after birth.

Living in Colonies

Feral cats tend to group up and live in colonies. Generally, they are all related and the colony will occupy and defend the area in which they live. For example, they may find a restaurant or a kind-hearted person who puts food out for them. The colony will keep that spot and keep it clear of others. Interestingly enough, humans in the area may not even realize the cats are there. These cats do all they can to avoid interaction with humans and become experts at staying hidden.

Trap-Neuter-Return Programs (TNR)

Some people and communities are strongly against feral cat colonies, even if those colonies are being cared for under a Trap-Neuter-Return (TNR) program. They may feel that wildlife is endangered by these feral cats.

The cat population is bursting at the seams and there is a growing need across the country for community-wide TNR programs. TNR is a non-lethal program. Spaying and neutering is a main piece of this program. If implemented correctly, these programs prevent more and more cats from being born into a very tough existence on the streets. These programs also ensure the care of these cats and improve their health and quality of life.

Overall, many feral cats don't survive. If they do survive, their lives are not easy without human caretakers. If you have feral cats in your area, get involved. Trap-Neuter-Return Programs do work and can be the solution for many urban and rural situations. Visit Alleycat Allies website at www.alleycat.org to learn how to start a program in your area.

Trap-Neuter-Return programs are one way to keep the feral cat population under control.

dealing with aggression

Topics:

A Natural Behavior

All animals, including cats, display aggression. It is a natural behavior they use for survival or to ward off a perceived threat.

This can be directed at people, other cats or animals. Unfortunately, if unprovoked or if it seems to be inappropriate, it is not a behavior you want in your pet. Aggression displays in cats range from hissing to violent attacks. All aggressive displays should be taken seriously.

Most aggressive displays are due to your cat being defensive. There are very few animals in the world that attack without provocation. There are many types of aggression and a correct diagnosis is paramount. This should only be done by your veterinarian, a veterinary behaviorist, or an animal behavior specialist.

It is important to note the information provided here on aggression does not replace a professional consultation with a behavior specialist.

Diagnosing and Treating Aggression

In some cases, medical conditions can contribute to aggression.

Your cat should have a thorough physical examination and blood analysis within three months of a behavior consultation. This is needed to rule out any medical condition that may be contributing to the problem behavior. A behavior consultation will help determine in what circumstances the pet is aggressive and whether the aggression is toward family members, strangers, other pets in the household or strange pets.

Keeping a diary is the best way to ensure an accurate record of aggressive displays. This will also help determine if treatment is decreasing the occurrences. Behavior modification techniques or changes to the pet's environment may be necessary to modify aggression problems.

Aggression is most often a defense, used when provoked. It can be directed toward family members, strangers or other pets in the household.

Types of Aggression

Fear Aggression

Fear aggression arises when a cat is exposed and reacts to a perceived threat or stimuli. Situations previously associated with an unpleasant experience can also trigger fear aggression. Many cats may try to escape the area, hide or climb up high where it is safe when they are fearful. If prevented from escaping because they are cornered, they are likely to fight. The best way to approach a fearful cat is in a calm, confident and friendly manner. This is likely to be met with a less fearful response. Fear aggression toward family members might arise out of punishment or other unpleasant experiences associated with them. It is best to avoid any verbal or physical correction.

Aggression is necessary for survival, but when that aggression is misplaced or excessive and causing harm to you or other animals, it is not acceptable.

Aggression is a serious issue and you should seek help immediately at the first signs of any aggressive behavior.

Play Aggression

Play aggression could be a contradiction in terms. When your cat or kitten is playing, he is having fun and his body language would not be that of a defensive cat. He may grab, bite, and chase, but these behaviors can be redirected into more appropriate ones. See Chapter 8.

Territorial Aggression

Territorial aggression is usually exhibited toward other cats that approach or reside on your property. It can also be directed at people or other animals. This can happen when you bring another cat into the house, or when the cats have been living together quite happily and one reaches social maturity at one to two years of age. These sudden changes may cause fear or anxiety.

Note: Territorial aggression often occurs in conjunction with fear aggression.

When a new cat is brought into the family, the resident cat may exhibit territorial aggression.

Types of Aggression *Continued*

Pain-Induced Aggression

When you are in pain, the last thing you want anyone to do is touch you where you hurt. Even if your cat is not exhibiting pain, certain medical conditions may make him more irritable and prone to aggression. Fear and anxiety further compound many of these cases. Unfortunately, once your cat learns aggression is successful in making you go away, it may recur when similar situations arise in the future, whether or not the pain is still present.

Maternal Aggression

Maternal aggression occurs when a cat is protecting her babies. This can be modified by using desensitization and counter-conditioning techniques. Along with highly motivating rewards, it may be possible to train your cat to accept handling of her kittens.

Redirected Aggression

Redirected aggression arises out of other forms of aggression and is defined when the cat is aggressive toward something else. When she can't take her aggression out on the "something else," she takes it out on what she can get to—you or another cat or pet in the home. It is important to identify and treat the initial cause of aggression and prevent exposure to the causes that triggered the aggression. It is likely to occur when the cat is aroused at the same time you or another pet is approaching. Cats that are highly aroused must be avoided until they calm down.

Petting-Induced Aggression

Some cats bite while being petted, while others are intolerant of all handling. Most cats with petting aggression accept a certain amount of petting, but then become highly agitated and attack when they have had enough. This can be difficult to understand, since many of these cats seek attention and seem to enjoy physical contact from the owner for awhile.

It seems these cats have a certain threshold for the amount of physical interaction they can tolerate. First, identify and avoid responses that might increase your cat's fear or anxiety. Make all handling experiences positive. When handling, physical restraint must be avoided, as cats that are placed in a position where they feel constrained or unable to escape might become aggressive.

Social Status Aggression

Information on the social structure and relationship between cats is continually being updated with new research. Cats do maintain social relationships when living in groups, leading to the speculation that some form of social structure exists.

Assertive displays may be displays of social status, such as soliciting attention through attacks or biting, aggression during petting, attempts to control the environment by blocking access to doorways, refusing to be moved from sleeping areas, stalking family members and threats or aggression to owners when walking or passing by the cat.

Cats have a social hierarchy system in which they live and social structures are often maintained with aggressive displays and actions. Some cats may show aggression toward their owners or other cats when displaying assertiveness and protecting their resources. These resources could be a favorite sleeping place, couch or even you. Since cats are known to be a social species, it is not surprising that some cats will assert their authority or leadership when challenged by a subordinate cat or family member in the home.

When a cat in the household dies, there will be a shift in the social standings as the cats adjust and reset the rules of who has what. You may even find a once-shy cat steps up and claims something he previously was not strong enough to challenge the other cat for.

Learned Aggression

When a cat learns aggression is successful at removing the perceived threat, it is likely the behavior will reoccur or escalate because the aggression has been rewarded. Some forms of aggression are inadvertently rewarded by owners who, in an attempt to calm the pet and reduce aggression, actually encourage the behavior with patting or verbal reassurances. Pets that are threatened or punished for aggressive displays may become even more aggressive.

Resource Guarding

Resource guarding is exactly what it sounds like. "I will defend something I find valuable." This may be as simple as pushing another cat away from a food bowl. The other cat defers, because it is not as important to the second cat as it is to the first. Unfortunately, some of these situations may turn into a full-blown fight. It depends on the cats.

Mewsings
Guarding Food

Resource Guarding

Mick says: I have a cat who will continually force any one of my five cats away from a dry food bowl when he hears another cat eating. So I now have five food bowls placed around my home, including one inside a cat tree. When a cat is eating there, his butt blocks the opening, and my cat who is guilty of resource guarding can't get to the bowl. Also, with five bowls, there are too many to guard all at once, so he gives up. This same cat will defer and walk away from all the other cats, including our new kitten, if I put down wet food.

Stimulating Your Cat's Senses

The goal of enrichment is to provide your cat with variety during her day and night.

Enrichment should reduce stress as well as introduce change into a stagnant environment. An environment that doesn't change could become boring and create stress. Things used to improve your cat's life should be easy to physically move, clean and be fun for your cat.

Cats need more to do than lie around and sleep all day. They need toys and diversions that will stimulate and enrich their lives, just like humans.

Think of things that will stimulate your cat's sense of sight, sound, smell and touch. Don't try to cover all the senses at once. You don't want to give your cat sensory overload. Anything you do to enrich your cat's world should be done in increments so she doesn't become confused or stressed. For example, if you were playing a new video game and had to start at level 10, you might try it once and never want to touch it again because it was too hard from the start.

There are four areas of your cat's life where you can provide enrichment—environmental, social, training and natural.

Cats need toys, playtime and a changing environment to enhance their lives. Birdie loves to play "fetch" with silk flowers.

Environmental Enrichment

Make Feeding More Complex

Rather than providing food in a bowl, try stuffing food into a Kitty Kong™ or treat ball. Use an empty tissue box and put food inside. Be sure the opening is big enough so your cat's head does not get stuck. Free-feed your cat by placing dry food around the house and letting her use her natural hunting instinct to find it.

This will help in situations in which your cat gets you up at night because she is hungry. It is also a great way to encourage active behavior. Be sure your cat is getting enough to eat when using one of these methods.

Encourage active behavior by placing your cat's food in a Kitty Kong™.

Toys and Games

Most cats are attracted to things that move. Soft toys, particularly those on the end of strings are often great fun. It is important to rotate toys so the cat does not become bored with the same toys all the time. Try a toy box, and vary the toys the cat has access to each day.

There are many game options, and it is a matter of finding out what interests your cat. Games that involve chasing and movement are quite popular.

There are also CDs and DVDs you can put on your computer screen or television during the day when you are gone. These are made especially for cats and show images of birds, fish and other fun things for the cat to sit and watch.

Refer to Chapter 10 for more information on cat toys.

Images of fish moving on a computer screen can keep a cat entertained while you are gone.

enrichment for cats

Environmental Enrichment *Continued*

Interacting With the Outside World

Providing your cat with access to the outside world is important. This can be offered in several ways, including a view out several windows or by having a secure outdoor play enclosure. Several companies make these types of enclosures that provide a safe and fun outdoor area for cats.

Providing your cat with "Window TV" is a great way to keep her entertained while providing additional mental and emotional enrichment. Cats love to look out a window and watch birds at bird feeders or birdbaths. Place one of these items by a window your cat can easily see out. She will watch the birds for hours.

Your cat can be trained to walk on a secure cat harness and lead. You can then take her outside into the garden for fully supervised play.

You should never let your cat out without supervision and fitted harness and leash. It is dangerous outside for a cat. See chapter 15 for more information.

Vertical Space Is Important to Cats

Cats love climbing and having access to high places, so it is good to create climbing areas and resting places at different levels around the house. This is especially beneficial if you have more than one cat. Building staircases, ramps and levels around a room of your house for climbing is another great way to enable them to be at different levels. Scratching posts can also satisfy your cat's desire to scratch and climb.

Cats love to look out windows and watch the birds at a feeder or birdbath.

Cats love to climb. Make sure they have access to a variety of climbing levels in your home.

Bring the Outside In

Bring a novel smell inside, like grass clippings placed in a small bag. If you bring plants into the home, be sure they are not toxic to your cat. Find a list of plants that are toxic to cats at www.landauercorp.com or www.arl-iowa.org

An indoor garden can be fun to explore, scratch and nibble. Plants and seeds of catmint, catnip and cat grass are available from pet shops and garden centers. Be sure your cat reacts in a positive way when using catnip.

Social Enrichment

Cats are social animals and need to have social interaction during their day. You can provide social interaction by petting, handling, play or just hanging out together on the sofa.

Interaction with another cat or dog in your home is also a wonderful way to allow them to be social. That is why having more than one pet is often beneficial to cats.

Shelters, such as the ARL, have developed programs to promote double cat adoptions. We believe it is in the best emotional and physical interest of the cat for her to have a friend. Two or more cats keep each other company and will play and interact. Shelters like the ARL have a "bonded buddy" program to adopt pairs of cats that came into the shelter together.

Mewsings
Catnip

Personality Changes

Question: "I take my cat, Bunny, outside on a harness/tether in the spring and summer. I work in my part of the garden while Bunny plays in her part which has a large patch of catnip. When we come back in, Bunny becomes angry and attacks me. I don't know why she's acting like this."

Answer: Some cats see personality changes around catnip. Bunny was becoming over-stimulated by the catnip. When they went inside, Bunny was so geared up she would become aggressive with her owner. Limit the amount of catnip your cat gets at a time. One way to do this is to buy a catnip toy. Let your cat play with it for a set period of time, before you pick it up and put it in a drawer until later. Another idea is to get a catnip plant and break off some of the catnip to give to your cat in the desired quantity.

enrichment for cats

Your cat should have appropriate ways to
entertain herself while you are away.
Provide her with scratching, climbing
and playing areas. Adopting a friend for
your cat will provide her with the social
enrichment she naturally craves.

Training Enrichment

A huge myth is cats cannot be trained.
The truth is you can teach your cat to sit, to
come and even to walk in a harness. This
provides your cat with mental stimulation and
makes life more interesting.

All training should be positive and
rewards used for appropriate behaviors.
Visit www.arl-iowa.org for cat training ideas
and techniques.

Natural Enrichment

Natural enrichment can be defined as
anything your cat or kitten likes to do to
entertain herself without your being involved.

Provide your cat with areas and items to
express natural behavior. These natural
behaviors include rubbing, scratching,
climbing, chasing, hunting, running and
playing. Hang a toy for your cat to stalk, chase
and attack. These behaviors are as varied as
cats personalities. So watch your cat and learn
what she likes and help her release her
inner lioness.

Some happy endings
from the Animal Rescue League of Iowa

Tank & Bear

When we were back home in Iowa for the holidays, Michelle suggested we go and take a look at the cats at the ARL. I knew the second we walked in that we would be leaving with a cat. I was surprised to learn that cats thrive in pairs. As we walked through the cat area we saw four little kittens sleeping in their beds. As Michelle and I watched, we noticed the black cat (Tank) was the most ornery and least likely to settle down. The striped cat (Bear) looked as if he was rolling his eyes at Tank and Michelle wanted to meet them both. After 10 seconds in the room, I was sold and Michelle was out the door to sign the papers!

Tank loves water and is often spotted on the tub ledge, just out of reach of the shower spray. He has also developed a love of washing his paws in his separate paw-washing water bowl. He is also the resident escape artist who loves to run out the door and into the hallway of our apartment building. Tank has developed a major league game of fetch. He always knows where Michelle hides the new hair ties. Because of his love for hair ties he has become very proficient at opening bathroom drawers in search of his favorite fetch toy. Tank cannot resist the urge to tear up toilet paper or paper towels whenever we leave them out.

Bear is such a sweetheart. He is independent and a force at cuddling. He never passes up a chance to sit on our laps as we work on the computer or watch TV. He loves to have his nose rubbed and is always the first to warm up to visitors, usually by jumping on their laps. He is also probably the cleanest cat around and the first to run to the sound of the treat bag opening.

Tank and Bear are an investigative duo who love to sniff groceries, pounce on boxes and wrestle. They also enjoy a good game of chicken with the vacuum cleaner. There is no doubt these two are brothers as they can be found wrestling one moment and cuddling the next.

We have loved watching our kittens grow up and spending time with them.

The Bonnemas

Gone to a Good Home!

living with special needs cats

Topics:

Deaf Cats

Blind Cats

Deaf Cats

Living with cats that are deaf or blind may seem to be a challenge, but they are quite capable of living happy, normal lives.

Deaf cats should always be kept inside. They are not able to hear cars coming or other dangers.

Deaf cats hear in their own way. They have an extraordinary ability to feel the vibrations from walking, other animals or sounds such as an oven door closing or furniture being moved. Sometimes, because of this extraordinary ability, you may start to question if the cat is really deaf, has some hearing loss or is just fooling you.

If your cat is deaf, his ears will still flicker and move. Perhaps that occurs from the vibrations he feels or it may be a way for him to communicate to his humans and other pets in the house.

Some deaf cats are easily startled. If you have a deaf cat that startles easily, you may want to stomp on the floor to let the cat know you are coming.

Interestingly, deaf cats are sometimes the most vocal. Some deaf cats however, do not meow at all and are very quiet. Some meow loudly when playing or when they see a bird or something outside.

All cats have a need to be high in the air, but for deaf cats this need is more extreme. It is likely a security issue. They want to be able to see what is coming their way since they can't hear it. Make sure you give your cat places where he can be high—atop a cat scratching post, dresser or shelf in a closet.

Communicate with your deaf cat by learning some basic sign language. You can teach him by sign to "Come", "Get Off the Counter" or "No". Mouthing the words clearly at the same time reinforces what you want to

It is especially important for deaf cats to have perches high in the air. This allows them to see what is going on all around them and provides a sense of security.

communicate. Of course, your own body language and facial expressions will go a long way in telling him "Yes" or "No". You can also make up your own hand signals for messages to your cat.

Your cat understands affection by feel, as opposed to hearing the words. Pet your deaf cat as you would any other cat.

You need to provide a little more care with a deaf cat. For example, a hearing cat may jump up on a counter near a hot stove and you can easily shout "No!" or "Get down!" to him and he responds. With a deaf cat, you need to train him not to get on the counter or near a hot stove to begin with, because he won't hear your shouts of concern.

Blind Cats

If the owner takes care to provide a safe, stimulating environment, a blind cat or kitten can have a happy life. Because blind cats are often able to adapt so well, many owners do not realize their cat is blind for a considerable length of time.

The degree of blindness in cats varies from total to partial blindness (cloudy sight, ability to differentiate between light and shade, tunnel vision). This is similar to the way human blindness varies. With most cats, especially as they age, the loss of sight is gradual. The cat is able to adapt gradually which is why some owners don't realize their cat is going blind.

When a cat becomes blind suddenly, it is noticeable, as the cat may bump into things when he walks or meow more often because he is confused. He may also develop different behaviors until he learns to adjust. He may strike out in self-defense at sudden movements or at being

> ### Carol's cat
>
> I live with a deaf cat and he talks to me by meowing constantly.
>
> He is also the calmest, most laid back cat I have.
> Nothing startles him.
> He lives a peaceful life.

Cats that are blind or deaf should not be allowed outdoors. They are not able to see or hear the dangers around them.

Blind Cats *Continued*

touched or startled suddenly. Your cat may not want to leave one particular spot, like his sleeping area. He may stop using his litter box because he doesn't want to move from the spot he knows.

Blind cats tend to meow or vocalize more because they need to know you are near and need to be reassured.

Blind cats rely on scent and memory to find their way around, so keep furniture in the same place, and do not leave obstacles in unexpected places. If your cat is prone to bumping into furniture, try padding table and chair legs with old pillows or foam to reduce impact damage. While most blind cats soon memorize routes and distances, not all manage this feat and rely on bumping into their signposts. Whiskers become more important to blind cats to judge their proximity to an object. Fully blind cats may clamber onto things rather than jump, but many also memorize heights and distances.

Do not carry a blind cat around. This can disorient him, so if you must move him, place him somewhere he knows well, such as his feeding or sleeping area so he can easily get his bearings. Don't move his litter box or feeding areas as he needs to find them easily by memory. He may actually even use them as markers to know where something else is in relation to his litter box and food bowls. Don't put a blind cat onto raised surfaces as he will probably be disoriented and fall off.

Sound is also important to a blind cat. Noisy toys such as balls with bells inside them, a paper sack or a scrunched up paper ball will provide stimulation and become a sound he enjoys.

A blind cat is easily disoriented. Do not allow them outdoors to roam.

Make sure your cat is wearing a collar at all times that states his address and disability, in case he escapes. He should also be microchipped.

If he is allowed to roam freely and is chased by another animal, he may become lost or run into the path of traffic.

Because he relies so much on scent and sound, a lost blind cat will probably be unable to find his way home once he is beyond his normal territory. The best approach is to never take your blind cat outside.

— CAT FACT —

A cat uses her whiskers to measure distance from an object.

Brody

In June 2009 I convinced my husband to stop by the ARL so we could see the new shelter. Even though I desperately wanted a cat, I promised my husband that I only wanted to look and would not ask to bring a cat home.

Well, we fell in love with Brody, a four-year-old, front declawed male that was picked up as a stray. It only took Brody a couple days to settle in. By the end of the week he was jumping up on our bed at night and laying between us, just purring away. Since we do not have any children, Brody has his own bedroom with attached bathroom. When we have house guests, they stay in "Brody's room".

Brody was the poster child for a perfect first cat. Then in late December 2009 I caught him spraying on a wall. A good friend suggested I take him to the vet to rule out a medical condition, since many times spraying can be a symptom of urinary infections.

It turns out he did have an infection and was put on antibiotics. When antibiotics didn't work, an x-ray revealed a bladder stone the size of an olive. Poor guy had been suffering for months. Brody was such a tough cat that despite the pain, he never cried out when urinating or exhibited any other symptoms of having a stone. After surgery to remove the stone, Brody was put on a special diet to prevent any future stones. We feel blessed to have Brody. He was placed with us for a reason. Not every pet owner could afford surgery or special food. Luckily we can and today Brody is a very happy and healthy cat.

My husband and I have jobs that can be stressful. Yet all that stress goes away when we come home at the end of the day and Brody is waiting. When he hears the garage door, he comes to the back door to wait for us. He sits between the blinds and the glass meowing at us.

We are grateful for the work of the ARL and all animal shelters. I wish there was no need for shelters, but as long as they exist, I will continue to support them.

Thank you for providing our house with such an amazing cat. He makes our new house a real home.

Mickie and Brian

Topics:

To keep your cat from feeling isolated when you tend the baby, replace the door on the baby's room with a screen door.

Cats and Babies

Cats and babies can be a great combination. Despite what a lot of people believe, cats are social animals and love "their" people.

When a new baby is coming into the family there are things you can do to prepare your cat.

It is important to remember that babies and cats should never be left alone or unsupervised.

Before Baby Comes Home

- Set up the nursery early and let your cat explore the room. NEVER allow the cat in the crib. Crib covers are available and are the best way to ensure your cat stays out of the crib. You can also make the inside of the crib unattractive to the cat by filling it with cans of coins. When the cans move they will make a loud noise thereby making the crib an unattractive place to be for a cat.

- Replace the regular door of the baby's room with a screen door. This allows you to have the door shut, but since it is a screen your cat won't feel left out while you tend the baby. It also serves as a way to keep the door to the baby's room "open" while keeping the cat out.

- Purchase powders and baby oils you will be using for your baby. Leave them out and open to get your cat used to some of the "baby smells". Put some of the powder on you and others in the household so the cat gets used to his owners having this scent on them.

- Plan early and start setting aside time to play with your cat. For example, if after the baby is born you anticipate being able to play and spend one-on-one time with your cat in the morning before the baby gets up and at night after the baby goes to sleep, start now spending 10 minutes playing with your cat during those times. This will get your cat prepared for this being "his" time. Don't overcompensate before the baby comes and play with the cat all the time. Once the baby is here, you won't have that kind of time and the cat won't get the attention he was used to.

- Cats need many toys. Make sure the cat has lots of toys he can play with when you are busy. Remember, do not ever use your fingers or feet to play with your cat. Only use toys such as "fishing poles" or balls. See chapter 10.

- Place the litter box and food and water bowls where they will remain after the baby comes home. Locate them in places a crawling baby can't go. This way your cat can maintain his territory and not feel invaded.

- Tape the sound of a baby crying and start playing it off and on. This will familiarize your cat with the sound. Vary the times of day and night you play it so the cat gets used to the sounds at any time.

- Buy a toy doll that crawls and have it crawl around your house. Reward the cat with treats or praise when the cat interacts appropriately with the toy doll. Do not punish the cat if he reacts badly. Just remove the doll and try it again until appropriate behavior is demonstrated. Hold, rock and carry the doll as you would a baby. When the baby comes home, these actions will be familiar to your cat.

When Baby Comes Home

After the baby comes home, there are many things you can do to ease the transition for your cat.

- When visitors come to the house, have them pay attention to the baby and the cat if the cat wants attention.

- When the cat is in the room with the baby, give the cat treats and special attention.

You want to reward the cat with the things she likes whenever the baby is around. Do not punish the cat for inappropriate behavior, just remove the cat or the baby from the room. If you punish the cat, she will associate being punished with the baby and the cat's acceptance of the baby will take longer.

- Spend some one-on-one time with your cat.

- Try not to change your cat's routine.

- When the baby starts to crawl, walk or express an interest in the cat, teach your child not to poke at the cat or pull her tail.

Make sure your cat has a variety of toys to keep herself entertained while you are busy with the baby.

A doll you can hold and rock as if it were a real baby will help your cat become familiar with these activities.

Cats Can Move Too

At the Animal Rescue League, one of the saddest things we see is a family bringing their cat into the shelter because they are moving.

Cats can move with the family just like dogs or kids. If you are planning to move, make moving your cat as important as moving your children or television.

Help for Your Stressed Cat

Feliway® is a synthetic copy of the feline facial pheromone used by cats to mark their territory as safe and secure.

It is not a drug, so it doesn't have the potential side effects that drugs might. Feliway® is used with cats that are stressed or to help with aggression and spraying.

Moving to a New Home

Whether you are moving to another home in the same city or another state, a move can be stressful on your cat.

Cats are creatures of habit and like their lives with as little disruption as possible.

Cats react to changes in their surroundings at different levels. One may wonder what is up and be curious about all the packing and activity, while another may hide under the bed and be completely stressed. Your cat will accept the change and acclimate to her new home with understanding, love and patience from you.

Keep the following points in mind as you prepare to move.

Packing

- Close box lids as you pack so your cat doesn't get shut into one. Boxes can be toys for a cat.

- On moving day put your cat in a room that has been emptied and close the door. Put food/water, a litter box, bed and carrier in the room. Also, put something that smells like you in the room so your cat has your scent with her. Put a sign on the door instructing people to keep it closed and that the family cat is in the room.

- Put a collar and tags (including rabies and ID) on your cat. Have your cat microchipped prior to the move.

Inside Your Car

Have the following cat supplies in your car as you move.

- A carrier with food/water, a litter box and bed or blanket in it. Add a shirt or towel that smells like you. The carrier should be large enough for your cat to stand up, turn around and lie down comfortably.

- Plenty of water and food in case you need to refill

- Treats

- Litter and scoop

- Plastic bags for waste removal

- Bath towels or blankets to cover the carrier for additional warmth or during noisy, heavy traffic

- Paper towels and other wipes for any accidents

- Veterinarian's name and vet records

- Your name and contact information on the carrier, as well as an emergency contact

- Feliway® spray to help keep your cat calm during transit

- Favorite toys

- Confirm early with hotels that your cat can come into the room with you. Do not leave your cat alone in the car overnight. This will add to your cat's stress.

It is normal for some cats not to eat or drink very much when stressed. Monitor this when you get to your new home. If things are not back to normal within 24 hours, see a veterinarian.

When You Arrive at Your New Home

- Take the cat in the carrier into your new home as soon as you arrive.

- Place your cat in a room that will not be entered until everyone is gone. Open the door to the carrier.

- Put a sign on the door that tells everyone to leave the door shut.

- Put the belongings she traveled with in the room with her.

- The first night in your new house let your cat out to be around you after everyone has left. This will reduce his stress to see you and familiar things. Keep doors and windows without secure screens closed. You need to ensure your cat does not get outside.

A Few Other Tips

These few additional tips will help your cat make the transition to a new home more easily. Cats are amazingly resilient creatures and they enjoy new places to explore and new things to discover, as long as their beloved humans are with them.

- Keep a few pieces of unwashed clothing or towels with your cat when you get to the new home. They smell like you and will give your cat comfort.

- Move your cat on the same day you are moving. Do not take your cat to the new home one day and then move the next. Never leave your cat alone in an unfamiliar place.

- Talk to your cat in a soothing voice as you drive to your new home and are getting him set up in the new house.

- If you have more than one cat, move them all at the same time. The cats will soothe each other as they go through the moving process.

- Do not pick your cat up and force him out of the room you set up for him at the new home. Let him come out on his own.

- Do not change your cat's food.

- Do NOT let your cat outside at the new place even if she was allowed outside at the old house. She needs to learn this is her new home and where she belongs.

Anchor your Christmas tree to the ceiling with a plant hook.

Cats and Christmas Trees

You can have a Christmas tree and cat at the same time.

- Set up the tree and leave it undecorated for a few days. If you set the tree up without decorating it, she can get used to it being there. Once the tree is decorated, it isn't such a new adventure.

- Invest in a heavy-duty tree stand and make sure the tree is properly and safely secured it. You can add to the sturdiness of the base by attaching it to wood pieces. When you put a tree skirt around the base of the tree, no one will see the stand.

- Anchor your tree to the wall or ceiling. This is a great way to ensure the tree doesn't topple if your cat gets curious. Position the tree against a wall in front of a large picture. Remove the picture and secure the tree to the wall hook where the picture was hanging using fishing line and a strong hook. When you take the tree down, remove the fishing line and put the picture back.

You can also anchor your tree by placing it under a plant hanging from the ceiling by a hook. Remove the plant, and tie the tree to the ceiling plant hook with fishing line. After Christmas, put the plant back up.

Invest in a heavy-duty tree stand. Attach it to wood pieces for extra security.

Decorating Your Tree

- Leave the bottom third or fourth of the tree without decorations to begin. Once some of the decorations are on, wait a few days and add to the bottom area. The cat will have had time adjust to the sparkling decorations before you some in paw's reach.

- Do not use tinsel on your tree. Tinsel is very dangerous to cats, especially if swallowed.

- When you choose tree ornaments, consider types that won't be too tempting for your cat. Try to find ornaments that are heavier and don't dangle a great deal.

- Before putting the lights on your tree, coat the cords with Bitter Apple to prevent your cat from chewing on them. See Chapter 14.

- Thread any dangling cord through a piece of PVC tubing or cable cover to further prevent your cat from chewing the cord. Paint the tubing a dark green color so it is not as noticeable.

- Hang your ornaments with ribbon or decorative cording instead of ornament hooks. Ornament hooks can be very dangerous to cats or other pets if swallowed or chewed on. Coat the ribbon or decorative cording with Bitter Apple so your cat won't chew them. The ornaments can then be tied securely to the tree.

- If your cat shows an interest in the tree, place a corrugated cardboard scratching post nearby. You can also grow some "kitty greens" (cat grass or catnip) and place them near the tree. If you place items like these near the tree, the cat tends to be less interested in chewing or climbing the tree and more interested in the other attractions.

Some happy endings

from the Animal Rescue League of Iowa

Lelu

Living in the country, we are regularly visited by adult cats and kittens, puppies and dogs. While the adult animals may be strays, we think the kittens and puppies have been dumped in the hope they won't survive.

Lelu is one of the lucky kittens.

She found her way to our home one summer night. We heard the mewing and went outside to see a small, skinny, scared kitten about four months old. She was very fearful. She also was very hungry. She had no interest in coming close to strangers. We didn't know whether or not she was feral. Each night, we brought food to our garage to entice her inside and give her safe shelter. After about a week, we offered the food in our hand hoping she'd come close. In took some time, but soon, she did allow us to touch her, and a week later, she allowed stroking.

We set up a litter box in the garage that she started using right away. She became more confident and sociable.

After getting a clean bill of health from our vet, we put out the word that this pretty kitten needed a forever home. Michelle adopted lucky little Lelu. She now thrives happily in a family with three rescued cats and two rescued dogs.

Jeramy

Gone to a Good Home!

Absences from Home

If you are going to be gone for a few days you can leave your cat home alone.

In fact, most cats prefer staying home.

It is always a good idea to have someone check in on your cat if you are gone for more than two days to make sure he is eating, drinking, using the litter box and doing well emotionally.

Leave your contact phone numbers, as well as your veterinarian's, with the person who is checking on your cat. Notify your veterinarian's office that you will be gone and give them the name of the person who is checking on your cat.

Complete an authorization form and give it to your veterinarian. This will authorize the person caring for your cat to obtain veterinary care if needed.

Here are a few tips to make sure your cat is okay during your absence:

- Have a few feeding stations set up around your house so there is always plenty of food. If you have a cat that should be on a limited diet, use a feeder that has a timer and kicks out food at a set time. Have more than one of these so you have a backup should something go wrong with the automatic feeder. If you must use an automatic feeder, ask someone to stop in and make sure it has been working so your cat is being fed.

- Set out a few water stations and fill the bowls with fresh water right before leaving.

- Leave a radio on so your cat has noise somewhere in the house.

- Put a timer on a lamp so it goes on and off in the evening. This way your cat is getting some light and normalcy.

- Leave new toys for the cat to discover while you are gone.

If you only have one cat and are often gone for overnights or weekends, get a friend for your cat. This way your cat has company. Do not get a second cat and then head out of town, but rather find a time in your life when you will be home for a month to get them acclimated before you leave again. Your cat will appreciate having company while you are gone.

Most cats will prefer to stay home alone a few days as opposed to being boarded.

Grooming Your Cat

Cats have a built-in grooming brush on their tongues, which allows them to keep themselves neat and clean.

Cats will groom themselves several times a day, as they are typically fastidious animals. However, Persians and other long-haired cats need help from their owners with daily or weekly brushing sessions.

- Start brushing your kitten at an early age so she will get used to it and it will become a non-event. For cats you adopt as adults, start slowly with just a few brushes. Gradually make the grooming sessions longer. Brushing is good for your cat's coat as it removes dirt, spreads natural oils and prevents tangles. It can also be a great bonding activity.

- Keep grooming sessions positive. Never yell or raise your voice and never hold your cat down with force while you are trying to brush. Groom your cat when you are both relaxed. Sometimes offering treats or tasty food while you are brushing is a good way to connect being groomed with a positive experience.

- Touch your cat all over, including tail, back, feet, ears, belly, and head, so she gets used to it.

Brushing tips

- Use a metal comb. Begin at your cat's head and work your way down to her tail.

- Be gentle near chest and belly.

- Be careful around the eyes.

- If your cat has matted fur, you may want to go to a professional groomer or your veterinarian.

A cat's tongue has tiny barbs which make it a built-in grooming brush.

Always keep your cat or kitten's head up and out of the water during bathing.

Grooming Your Cat *Continued*

Bathing tips

Most cats will never need a bath, but if your cat has gotten into something smelly she will benefit from a bath.

- Have someone help you. Most cats don't like baths. Be careful holding your cat for a bath and talk to her in a soothing manner throughout the process. You want to minimize stress as much as you can.

- Use a shampoo made for cats.

- Place something in the sink or tub for your cat to stand on so she isn't continually slipping.

- The water should be lukewarm. For adult cats, fill the sink with three to four inches of water so she can keep her head and most of her body out of the water.

- Use a sprayer or plastic cup to thoroughly wet your cat. Be careful not get her ears, eyes, or nose wet.

- Gently massage in the shampoo and remember to keep speaking softly to your cat. Rinse with the sprayer or cup avoiding the eyes, ears and nose.

- Dry your cat with a soft towel.

- Giving treats after a bath reinforces the positivity of having a bath.

Use a soft towel to dry your cat off after a bath. Remember to treat and praise.

Nail clipping tips

- Touch your cat's feet when she is young so she is used to having her feet handled and touched. If you get a kitten, start clipping her nails early so she is used to it. Be sure to praise your cat or kitten when you touch her feet and give treats to her as you are doing it. You are associating touching her paws with getting good stuff.

- Apply gentle pressure to the top of your cat's foot and cushiony pad underneath. This will cause her to extend her claws.

- Use high-quality cat nail scissors (be sure they are sharp) to cut off the white tip of each nail, just before the point where it begins to curl.

- Be careful not to cut the "quick," a vein that runs into the nail. This pink area can be seen through the nail. If you do accidentally cut into this pink area, it may bleed. Apply styptic powder to stop the bleeding.

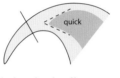

- Wrap your cat in a towel, if needed, to help control her other three legs as you are trimming.

- If you are nervous about doing this, ask your veterinarian to trim your cat's nails.

Wrapping your cat securely in a towel will help control the feet you are not trimming.

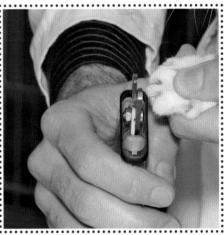

Apply pressure to the top and bottom of your cat's paw and her claws will extend.

Polydactyl Cats

Cats normally have five toes on their front paws and four toes on their back paws. Polydactyl cats may have 8 or more toes on each paw.

Polydactyl cats do not suffer any health problems in relationship to having extra toes and veterinarians do not consider it a deformity or a handicapping condition.

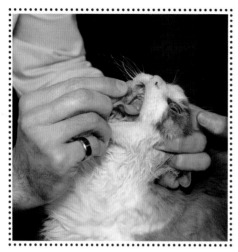

Tilt your cat's head back until her mouth opens to give her a pill.

Giving Your Cat a Pill

Giving your cat medicine, especially in the form of a pill, can be quite challenging.

If your cat is generally cooperative in nature, you can pill your cat by opening her mouth and simply dropping the pill down her throat.

Most cats are not as cooperative. Wrap your cat in a large towel so only her head protrudes. It works best to roll her in the towel and fold the end over her rear to prevent her from backing out of it. Hold the cat football-style or have her on a table facing you.

Using the hand of the arm holding the cat, grasp her head by placing your hand over her head with the thumb on one side and the middle finger on the other side just below the cheek bones. Tilt her head back until her mouth drops open slightly.

While holding her head securely in this position, grasp the pill with your other hand, using the thumb and forefinger. With the middle finger of the hand with the pill, press down on the bottom front teeth to open the mouth so you can see inside. Drop the pill in the V-shaped area at the back of her throat or place it there with your fingers. Quickly close the cat's mouth. You may want to blow gently in her face or stroke her throat to encourage swallowing. Let go and watch the cat for a few moments to make sure she doesn't spit out the pill.

A half-dropper of diluted chicken broth or water may make it easier for your cat to swallow the pill. If she spits out the pill, simply repeat the process. It may be necessary to switch to a dry pill if the initial one is sticking to your fingers. Don't throw the pill away. Simply allow it to dry and administer it another time.

Dangers Around the House

Houseplants

Keeping your cat out of plants can be a challenge. Some cats like to climb, bat at leaves, chew and get into the dirt and dig. Use a natural aversive to make the plant unattractive to the cat. If your cat is chewing on the leaves, put a substance, such as Bitter Apple, on the leaves or trunk. Check the label of anything you put on the plant to make sure it is safe for your plant and your cat.

Place decorative rocks or pinecones on top of the dirt to prevent digging in the soil. Keep in mind pinecones are light weight, so some cats may pick them up in their teeth or bat them around and out of the pot to play.

If your cat eats part of a poisonous plant, rush her to your veterinarian as soon as possible. Take the plant with you for ease of identification.

Some plants are poisonous to cats and must be avoided. In some cases, just parts of a plant (bark, leaves, seeds, berries, roots, tubers sprouts, green shells) might be poisonous. If you have any of these plants in your home, keep them safely out of your cat's reach.

Visit www.landauercorp.com or www.arl-iowa.org for a general list of plants that are known to be toxic to cats. If you have questions, or for a complete list, talk to your veterinarian.

BE CAREFUL!

Loose screens Make sure your window screens are securely in place so your cat cannot accidentally fall out a window.

Toilet cleaner and toilets Keep toilet lids closed so your cat or kitten doesn't jump up and into the toilet, especially if you use a cleaner that is automatically dispensed in your bowl upon flushing.

Sharp objects Be careful not to leave sharp objects, such as knives or scissors, on counters in case your cat decides to explore.

Hot stoves Do not leave your cat alone in the kitchen if the stovetop is hot. If he jumps onto the stovetop while it is hot he will not have time to react before the pads of his feet suffer burns.

Placing a plastic carpet runner, wrong side up, on counters or tables will deter your cat from jumping up without harming her.

Cats and Counters

Cats love to explore and are curious by nature, so they naturally jump on counters.

There are a few things you can do to keep cats off your counters.

- **Double-sided tape** Placing double-sided sticky tape on counters gives your cat an unpleasant experience without harming her. She jumps up and her paws become sticky from the tape, so she immediately jumps down. After a few tries the cat thinks the counter naturally feels this way.

- **Plastic carpet runner** This aversive has proven to be an effective way to keep cats off the counters. Turn the runner upside down so the pointed side is up. This will not hurt your cat, but most cats don't like the feel of it. If you keep the runner on consistently for a week, you can take it off and you should not need it again.

- **Orange** Many cats do not like the smell of orange. Use an orange cleaner that is safe for pets to clean your countertops. It will become a natural deterrent for your cat.

Mewsings
Sitting on a Piano

Question: "My cat Zip has developed the habit of jumping up on the piano. When he sees himself in the mirror above the piano, he meows and gets agitated while pouncing at the mirror."

Answer: As a way to get Zip off the piano, I suggested his owner place a piece of plastic carpet runner, turned upside down, on the piano. If he stays off the piano and away from the mirror, hopefully the problem will be solved.

Cats and Carriers

Getting a cat used to a cat carrier can be a challenge. She rarely leaves the safety of her home except to go to the veterinarian's office.

It is a good idea to get your cat used to being in a carrier since you do have to take her to a veterinarian. Additionally, you may need to travel or move with your cat, so having her as calm as possible in the carrier is good for both of you.

Set the carrier out with the door open. Let your cat sniff and inspect the carrier. Say "good cat" and walk away. All is good when the carrier is out in the house. Do not push your cat into the carrier, just let her be around it and inspect it. Add treats to the carrier. Let the cat sniff and find them and walk into the carrier to get the treats. Make the treats something your cat can't refuse.

After a couple of weeks, if the cat has shown interest and gone into the carrier to get the treats, start putting the cat in the carrier and shutting the door. Leave the cat in there with treats, for a few minutes and then open the door. While the cat is in there, say "good kitty" in a happy voice. Do this for a week or two. Put a favorite toy and towel in the crate, so it is soft and comfortable. You are making the carrier a happy place for the cat. The cat gets to go in and get tasty treats, hear praise, and then gets to come out. All is good in the cat's world.

Take the cat in the carrier for a short car ride, back in and out of the driveway. Take the carrier and cat back into the house and let your cat out of the carrier. Gradually lengthen the time the cat is in the carrier and traveling in the car. You are showing her that being in the carrier and in the car doesn't necessarily mean a trip to the vet.

Continue with treats while your cat is in the carrier and when she gets home and out of the carrier. All the trips and times in the carrier get the cat good things—treats, praise, and out of the carrier in a short time.

Over time, your cat will start to look at the carrier and car rides as an okay thing. When you have to take your cat to the veterinarian, provide treats while at the veterinarian's office as well. You are making even the trip to the veterinarian a good thing.

When taking your cat out of the carrier, it is best to open the door and let the cat walk out on her own. If she won't come out, gently reach in while talking to your cat and bring her out.

Remember to only open the door to the carrier when your cat is safely in your house or the veterinarian's office. Cats can get stressed, so opening the door to the carrier outside or when the room isn't secured is not safe for your cat.

Traveling with Your Cat

Ensure the safety and well-being of your cat when traveling.

Never travel with your cat loose in the car.

Cats can get under your feet or climb on you and cause visual or movement issues. Be sure to travel with your cat safely in a cat carrier.

For short distances, use a cat carrier. For longer distances, use a large dog crate and include a litter box, cat bed, toys, food and water. See Moving to a New Home on pages 126-127 for supplies and tips on traveling long distances with your cat.

Never open the crate door until you have the cat secured inside a house or room. Keep in mind traveling is stressful on a cat, and you don't want to open the car or kennel door and have your cat escape out onto the road or unfamiliar territory. Have a break-away collar and tags on your cat, along with a cat harness. Reach into the kennel and clip a leash onto the harness before you open the door. This way, you will have control of your cat the minute you open the door. Do not leave the leash on the cat in the carrier. You do not want your cat to get tangled in it.

Traveling tips

- Have current photos of your cat from different angles, so you can use them if she does escape.

- Have all vaccinations current when traveling and have your veterinarian records with you.

- Have your cat microchipped. A microchip is a permanent form of identification. Be sure you have your microchip registered.

- If your cat is on medication, take it with you. Include some extra days worth, just in case something detains you from returning home as planned.

- Take your cat's food with you, so you can keep her on the same diet. Take extra food and include treats for positive reinforcement.

- Put a t-shirt or other item that smells like you in the crate with the cat when traveling.

- If your cat has a favorite toy, take it along.

Some happy endings
from the Animal Rescue League of Iowa

Callie

My cat's name is Callie and she was adopted from the ARL Main in the fall of 1998.

Callie was a gift from my high school boyfriend who was a volunteer at the ARL. She was a little Calico bundle of joy and immediately won over every member of my family. Because we had such a great success with Callie, all of my family's future pets were adopted from the ARL. It was also because of Callie that I started volunteering at the ARL and have continued to do so. I enjoy helping people adopt pets that will bring them as much happiness as Callie has brought to me.

Callie's life now is pretty purrfect. She is a spoiled only child who is spending her senior years in the West Des Moines area and enjoys spending time outside in her 'catio'. Callie truly means the world to me. She is so sweet and is always by my side. She brings so much happiness to my life.

Thank you ARL for helping me and others have such great success stories with such wonderful pets.

Meghan

Maude

I was at the ARL cleaning with the usual group that has cleaned every holiday for the last nearly 20 years so staff could have time off to be with their families. It happened to be Easter and I met a cat named Maude. She was an eight-year-old stray waiting to go up for adoption. Maude and I had an instant connection that day. I couldn't get her out of my mind and I said 'hi' to her every time I was at the shelter after that. I cleaned again on July 4th and Maude was still there waiting for a home. After the cleaning and feeding was done, I was walking away from her to go home and I had a feeling she was looking at me. I turned around to look over my shoulder at her. She was squeezed and leaning to the front of her cage just so she could watch me walk away. I went back and opened her cage. She head butted me and I whispered in her ear that I'd be back for her.

I drove home that day and started thinking about all the wonderful cats, like Maude, that had been at the ARL for so long waiting for a home and the idea for a Summer Cat Getaway program came to me. The first cat into the program was Maude. I thought at a minimum I could get her out of her cage and find her a home with one of my friends. She came to my house; and Tom and I ended up adopting her.

It just shows what a bond between a person and a cat can do. The Summer Cat Getaway program has helped over 100 cats so far. Over 64 of these adult, long term cats have already found homes in the three months since we started the program. Amazing. Maude will never know what she accomplished. But I will never forget the power of what a bond can do.

Carol

Gone to a Good Home!

other situations

Behavior and Physical Changes

Behavior changes

- ● sleep habits
- ● loss of interest in favorite activities
- ● separation anxiety
- ● depression
- ● eating patterns

Physical changes

- ● stomach upset
- ● hair-loss
- ● over-grooming

The surviving cats will need individual attention and reassurance. If the cats were sociable, the surviving cats may search or cry out. If they were unsociable or indifferent to each other, the survivors might simply rearrange themselves into a new hierarchy, dividing up their former companion's territory between them. Sometimes the surviving cats blossom if they were previously at the bottom of the pecking order. Let the surviving cats work the hierarchy out on their own.

Grief and Grieving Cats

Anyone who has loved and lost a pet knows the pain that comes with the loss. This is normal. Pets are a source of companionship, comfort, unconditional love and pure joy.

Many people wonder if their other pets will grieve the loss as well and the answer is yes, even though it may be subtle. Cats are aware that a familiar person or companion cat is absent. They will often look for that cat or human around the house. If there are multiple cats in the home, the death or absence may change an established hierarchy.

Grief is a reaction to the sudden absence of something or someone who caused happiness, satisfaction, comfort, or reassurance. Cats may become withdrawn at the loss or over-attached and "clingy" to their humans.

If you have a cat experiencing the loss of another pet, there are some things you can do to help.

- Spend extra time playing with your cat. Pet him a little more than you might have otherwise.
- Leave a radio or television on if he is home alone.
- When the time is right, adopt another pet. Make sure you choose a pet that is close in age and personality to your resident cat.
- Try not to change your cat's routine.
- Let the surviving cats in the household work out the hierarchy on their own.

Changes

When the family structure is disrupted by the death of a person or another pet, life changes for the surviving pets. For cats, whose sense of smell is better than humans, this includes the absence of particular scents.

Your Feelings May Affect the Cat

Cats are sensitive to changes in human emotions, behavior and routine. If you are upset, your cat will respond to this and may become anxious, depressed, agitated or physically unwell. If you are finding it difficult to come to terms with the bereavement, whether human or animal, you may find it helpful to talk to a pet loss hotline, your veterinarian or someone at an animal shelter that loves animals like you do.

When there has been a human death in the family, please remember to still make time for your pets. They depend on you, and you may find comfort in them being around during this difficult time.

Adopting a Cat Grieving a Loss of a Human

Sometimes a cat will end up at an animal shelter needing to find a new home when his human guardian has died or gone into a care facility. This is often worse for a cat that is grieving the loss of their owner, as well as the loss of their home and everything they knew. Adopters shouldn't expect such a cat to be playful and immediately fit in. Be tolerant and patient and allow the cat alone time. Always keep an eye on his eating habits and physical appearance.

Once your new cat has accepted you as the new caregiver, he may become clingy. Having lost one human in his life, he may not want to let you out of his sight. If you are away from home during part of the day, you could leave a recently worn article of clothing about the house so the cat can smell you.

Alternatively, he may remain aloof. Don't press attention on an unwilling cat, but spend time in the same room and talk to him. Encourage him to interact with you. The settling-in process may take longer, so be patient.

Mewsings
A Grieving Cat

Another cat?

Question: "I had two cats, Gizmo and Shirley. Shirley passed away and Gizmo is alone for the first time in ten years. Should I get another cat for Gizmo?"

Answer: I talked to Gizmo's owner about the need to let him go through the grieving process of losing Shirley before deciding whether to get another cat or not.

When cats are grieving, it is good to spend extra one on one time with them, especially when they are older cats like Gizmo. Sometimes turning on a radio or television when you are going to be gone helps to give them some background noise so they do not feel so alone.

When Gizmo starts to return to normal, his owner can consider getting a second cat. The gender shouldn't be the issue when choosing a cat, but rather the age. For a friend for Gizmo, getting an older cat would definitely be the way to go. They will want to do the same kind of activities.

Myths About Cats

There are many unfortunate myths and misinformation about cats being circulated.

Myth: Black cats are bad luck. In Japan, black cats are considered good luck.

Myth: Cats always land on their feet. It is true that cats instinctively fall feet first, but they may also break bones and incur other injuries.

Myth: Cats should drink milk every day. People tend to believe cats love milk and need milk for their diet. It is true they tend to like milk, but they do not need it for proper nourishment. We suggest that you do not give your cat milk at all.

Myth: Cats get their balance from their whiskers. Cats use their whiskers to feel, not for balance.

Myth: If you are pregnant, you need to get rid of your cat. Sadly, hundreds of cats are relinquished to animal shelters every year because of this myth. It is true some cats can be infected with a disease called toxoplasmosis, which occasionally can be spread to humans through litter boxes and cause serious problems in unborn babies. However, these problems can be controlled if the expectant mother avoids contact with the litter box and assigns daily cleaning to a friend or other family member. Personal hygiene, such as frequent hand washing, is an important factor in preventing transmission. If you are concerned, talk with your doctor.

Myth: Cats may try to suffocate babies. Cats may try to get into a crib with a baby because it is new or warm or smells good. But there is no intent on the part of a cat to suffocate or steal the breath from a baby. See Cats and Babies on page 124 for more information.

Myth: Cats are aloof. Cats can tend to be aloof and more standoffish at first, but cats will absolutely bond with their caretakers and ultimately their owners.

Myth: If a cat is injured, it can lick its wounds and the wounds will heal automatically from their saliva. Actually, licking can slow the healing process and cause more issues. If your cat is injured, he needs to see a veterinarian.

Myth: Cats are unhappy if they are kept indoors. For cats that are used to being outside, there may be an adjustment period when keeping them inside all of the time, but it can be done. One key is never to let them outside again and give them access to windows to look out, provide them with plenty of toys and companionship inside the house. Inside cats live much longer and healthier lives than outside cats. Refer to Chapter 15 for more information on keeping cats happy inside.

Myths About Cats *Continued*

Myth: **Cats don't really like people and don't need a lot of care.** Cats may appear to be independent in nature, but the truth is cats are social creatures and require care just like any other pet. Cats tend to live longer because of the level of care we are able to provide for them. More cats are being treated like members of the family and form strong bonds with their humans.

Myth: **All cats should have a litter of kittens before you spay them.** Spaying a cat will help prevent such things as mammary cancer, ovarian cysts, complications of pregnancy, including stillbirth and malformed kittens. There is no medical or behaviorial reason your cat should have a litter of kittens before being spayed. The reality is some people just don't want to spend the money to have their cat spayed, so they sometimes make an excuse to avoid doing it.

The cat over-population in the country is out of control and unacceptable. It is important to spay or neuter your cat.

Myth: **Cats and dogs hate each other.** Unfortunately, the entertainment industry has helped to perpetuate this myth. The reality is cats are totally capable of affectionate and close relationships with dogs. Pets form relationships with other pets and seem to understand they are all part of the family.

Cats and Collars

If your cat has never worn a collar, it is best to introduce her to it in small steps.

This way she won't see the collar as a threatening or bad thing.

Use a breakaway collar on your cat. If the collar gets caught on something and your cat pulls, it will break apart. Cats can get caught on things outside as well as inside so make sure you only use these types of collars.

Let your cat sniff the collar. Put the collar on her while giving her treats. Leave the collar on for 15 seconds. Remove the collar while petting her and giving treats.

The next day repeat the process, leaving the collar on for 30 seconds. Continue the steps every day, leaving the collar on a little while longer each time until she doesn't mind it and you can leave it on full time.

Your cat may have no adverse reaction to the collar, in which case you can leave it on her. Keep her confined until she becomes used to the collar and isn't trying to get it off. Add a tag with your name and phone number, so if your cat gets lost she can be returned.

If you have a kitten, monitor the size of the collar as she grows so you can ensure it is big enough.

other situations

Mewsings

Water Bowl Issues

Question: "My cat Jack splashes water out of his water dish and all over the floor. I am tired of constantly cleaning up the mess."

Answer: Some cats think this is a fun game. There are a few things you can do in this situation. Putting a couple bowls out with just a little water in them will help. This way, you won't have a big pool for Jack to play in. You can also put a few rocks in the bottom of the water bowl before adding water. Jack may not like the look of the bottom of the bowl as much without a reflection to play in.

Chewing Furniture

Question: "My cat Max is one year old and recently started chewing on a leather chair. How can I get him to stop doing this?"

Answer: I suggested Max's owner visit the vet to make sure there is not a food issue. She should also cover the chair with Bitter Apple spray or another unpleasant substance. Make sure it won't harm the leather. Max likely will decide the chair isn't fun anymore and will stop chewing. I also suggested she get Max some toys with different textures to chew on. Refer to Natural Aversives in chapter 14.

Toilet Paper

Question: "My two adult female cats have discovered the toilet paper roll. They have decided it is fun to unroll the entire thing while I sleep. The cats, Meg and Maude, are two-year-old sisters."

Answer: First, shut the bathroom door at night or remove the toilet paper from the roll for a week or so. The cats will become bored and seek other play things. Supplement with lots of toys. The cats' owner can also make the toilet paper not as fun by putting something bad smelling or tasting on it. Bitter Apple spray is safe and works great.

Mewsings

Dog Doors

Question: "My cat Dexter uses the dog door to get outside. Dexter and the dog like each other a lot, so he enjoys following him."

Answer: This is quite a challenge, because if a cat doesn't like a loud noise every time he comes close to the dog door, chances are the dog won't either. Smell is a different thing. Some cats hate the smell of citrus/orange, so putting orange near the dog door can be a natural deterrent. Dogs, on the other hand, don't seem to have that issue. This worked with Dexter. Nancy put cut-up oranges in a container near the door and the cat didn't go close to it. He hated the smell of orange.

Free-Feeding

Question: "I have three inside cats, all about four years old. I feed them once in the morning and once at night in one central location. All my cats occasionally vomit after they eat and I'm worried. There doesn't seem to be a medical reason for this."

Answer: We talked about free-feeding the cats—in other words, leaving dry food out for them all the time, so they can eat when they want. We also discussed setting up different feeding locations around the house. All three cats were hungry in the morning, and had limited food all in one location. They would eat quickly without chewing or digest it properly, causing them to get sick.

The cats' owner set up three different feeding locations in the house and left food out for them at all times. After a time the cats figured out there was going to be food available all the time and the vomiting stopped.

clicker training your cat

Topics:

What Is Clicker Training?

Clicker training is an "operant conditioning" method used for training.

You are using the science of learning and applying it to your cat by using a clicker as a marker for behavior.

The clicker training method uses positive reinforcement. It is reward-based and a humane method of training. This method allows your cat to rapidly identify the behavior you desire.

At least one study has shown that the clicker can reduce training time by one-third. Tasks learned with the clicker are retained even years after the fact and with no additional practice after the initial learning has taken place. This is probably due to the fact the animal participates fully in the learning process and applies himself to it. This learning retention is present in all positive reinforcement training, but does not regularly happen with correction-based training.

Cats can be trained to sit and come, as well as other behaviors. Clicker training uses positive reinforcement to get the behavior you desire from your cat.

Why Clicker Train?

There are many methods of training your cat.

The most humane, effective and scientifically-based training method is using a bridging stimulus commonly known as clicker training.

The advantage of using the clicker is you can mark the exact behavior you want, similar to pushing the button on a camera and looking at the picture. It allows you to say, "yes, that is what I wanted" and then you can reward.

The clicker also is non-emotive, so your tone of voice doesn't come into play when training, which can be a huge benefit if things are not going the way you want. At first, the clicker means nothing and will have to be paired with a high-value reward.

There is the belief that when you click there is a dopamine (feel-good chemical) release in the brain. Another way to put it is if you really like soda, when you hear the sound of the drink being opened. you get that ahhhhhhhhh effect in your head even before you take a sip.

As you train, still use a word, such as "good", to reward your cat because over time you can fade the clicker and treats out of training.

Some cats may be fearful of the click. Before you start, click from a distance and watch your cat's reaction. If she is afraid of the click, you may want to use a "mouth click," a similar noise made by you or a short word that you do not necessarily use in conversation, like "bing".

If your cat will not take a treat from your hand, place it on a plate instead. You can also gently throw the treat to your pet.

Desirable Behavior

If your cat is doing something you don't like and you interrupt her and get her to do something you do like, make sure you wait a minimum of three to five seconds before rewarding the desired behavior. You do not want the cat to think she is being rewarded for both the undesirable and desirable behaviors.

clicker training your cat

How to Use a Clicker

Determine what motivates your cat.

Treats are generally the best motivator and should be soft and moist and approximately the size of a one-fourth-inch cube.

1. Find a quiet location with no distractions, if possible.

2. Have treats in one hand and the clicker in the other.

3. Click and treat right away. Do this five or six times and then stop.

4. Wait for your cat to look away and then click. If she looks back at you, you know your clicker has meaning. If she doesn't look back at you, repeat this step.

5. This will be the one and only time you click for attention. Once this is done, you are ready to train.

How training works:

1. Get the desired behavior.

2. Mark the behavior (click).

3. Reward the behavior. If you click, you must reward with a treat.

If at any time you see your cat doing something you like and you don't have a clicker or treat, you still need to let her know she has done a good job. Any behavior that is rewarded is more likely to re-occur.

How Do I Teach My Cat?

In case you are skeptical, it is possible to train your cat.

There are several techniques you can use to get the desired behavior.

All the techniques are "hands off". In other words, there is no need to grab, push or pull your cat to teach her the things you want her to know.

Luring

The luring method guides the cat through a behavior. For example, place a treat in front of the cat's nose, move the treat back toward the cat's ears slowly. When the cat is in a Sit position, click and treat without telling her to sit. At this point, your cat has no idea what the word means, so you want to teach the position before you put a word to it. Repeat three or four times using the treat but still no verbal cue. Remember to click as she does the behavior. Do it two or three times and say "sit," so your cat associates the word with the action.

Now it is time to get the behavior without a treat in your hand. Use the same hand action you were using when you were teaching your cat to sit. At the same time, say "sit." When she does it, click and treat. Now your cat knows what that word means, and you only need to use the treat to pay after you click.

Targeting

Targeting is teaching your cat to touch with some part of his body. For example, you could teach your cat to touch the tip of a pen or your finger with her nose. Then use that tool to move your cat into whatever position you like. Where the head goes, the body follows.

When teaching a "target," the first step is to present the target to your cat just in front of her face. She has a maximum of three seconds to touch it. If she doesn't, remove the target and place it a bit closer.

Anytime your cat touches the target, "click" and treat. Once she gets the idea, start moving the target around. Teach your cat to move around to get to it. If at any point it was going well and the cat is unsure, you may have moved the target too far away too soon. Break it down into smaller steps.

Capturing a Behavior

To capture a behavior you watch and wait, and when the desired behavior happens, "click" and treat. This technique should be used sparingly and only if you cannot lure or target the desired behavior. At first, your cat won't know what she was "clicked" for and could become stressed.

Modifying Behavior

Clicker training is a fantastic way to tell your cat she is doing the right thing. Unfortunately, people wait for their cat to do something wrong and correct it. That is like letting your child run out on the road and then dragging her back and telling her it was wrong.

Training is all about being proactive and not reactive. Look for the good and reward it. Remember you get what you pay for.

Training Tips

All training sessions should be short, sharp and fun.

Do not train to the point where your cat is bored or disinterested. If you do this, her last memory of training won't be good and you don't want that. If you find you are becoming frustrated or upset, end the training session and try again later.

- All family members need to be consistent.

- Try not to teach too many behaviors at once. Focus on teaching the basic behaviors well before moving on to more complex exercises.

- Teach your cat the desirable behaviors you want.

- If your cat does not do the behavior on your request, it is probably because you have not taught them well enough.

- Practice.

- Every time you interact with your cat, you are teaching her something. Try to make sure each interaction is an appropriate one.

- Finish each session while the cat still wants more. Remember some cats have a short attention span and are easily distracted or fatigued.

cat body language

Topics:

Understanding Cat-Speak

We wish our cats could tell us how they feel and what they need and actually they do.

We just have to learn to talk cat.

A cat's main method of communication is through body language.

A cat also uses some vocal communication because our cats know it will get our attention.

The great thing about cats is they act how they feel and feel how they act. They have no reason to lie, so if they want a pat, they will let you know. The same goes for when they are upset or frightened. We just have to learn to listen.

Of course, we have to know what we consider normal. The more you observe your cat, the better you will be at reading her body language.

> — **CAT FACT** —
> Watch the hair on your cat's body. It will stand up evenly all over the body when she is scared.
>
> When she feels defensive or threatened and getting ready to attack, the hair stands up along the spine and tail.

Body Language Signals

Relaxed cat: Some of the body language your cat displays when she is relaxed involves a soft, relaxed body free of muscle tension and whiskers in a neutral position. The tail will be in a neutral position, and the eyes may be squinting and blinking regularly. In many cases, she may be purring. However, it is good to remember that some cats purr when they are stressed.

Fearful cat: When frightened, a cat will likely try to hide and escape. If she feels threatened and can't escape to a safe place up high or under something, she may show some or all of the following:

- Muscles tensed ready for flight or fight
- Eyes fixed on the threat and pupils dilated
- Crouched down
- Ears flattened, tail low and chin drawn in

If the cat rolls on her side or back while showing the above signs, stay away. This is your last warning before the teeth and claws come out.

Defensive cat: A defensive cat believes she has little choice but to defend herself. You may just be trying to be friendly, but the cat's perception may be different. The cat may exhibit the same characteristics as a fearful cat.

Stimulated cat: This may occur when you are playing or petting your cat. She may become stimulated, which is generally a good thing, and it means the cat is having fun. Be sure the cat does not become over-stimulated. Look for these signs:

- Face tightened
- Vocalization
- Fur is fluffed up
- Tail flicks back and forth

> **When looking at your cat's body language, don't rely on only one communication signal.**
>
> Look at the whole cat, as well as the environment around you. Is there anything that may be causing a change in your cat's behavior? It is important to look at all behaviors in context.

When your cat is relaxed her body will be free of muscle tension and her eyes may squint.

— CAT FACT —

Cats show contentment by using a kneading motion. This action is often accompanied by purring.

Body Language Signals *Continued*

Decoding your cat's emotions

There is a lot to observe when decoding your cat's emotions. Just like anything else we learn, it takes time. Most of us know when our friends or family members get upset. After some observation and time you should be able to interpret your cat's signals.

Causes of emotional distress

- Changes in physical environment.

- Anything that acutely startles the cat, such as loud noises.

- Unpredictable and unfamiliar manipulations or handling.

- Lack of choices or control over situations.

- Irregular and unpredictable feeding times. For example, cats are kept hungry for extended periods.

- Irregular and unpredictable cleaning of litter boxes.

- Absence of stroking, petting or other positive interactions with humans.

- Changes in social environment (new baby, roommate, change in owner's work schedule).

- Lack of mental stimulation.

Indicators of emotional distress

- Increased hiding or attempts to hide.

- Decreased social interaction.

- Decreased grooming.

- Decreased active exploration and play behavior.

- Greater proportion of daily time spent awake (exhibiting vigilance and scanning behavior).

Ever wonder why your cat jumps on the lap of the guest that doesn't like cats?

It is because people who don't like cats will do things cats like during greetings.

They squint their eyes, turn their heads and avoid direct contact with the cat. The cat's view is these people are saying hello and being non-threatening, and, sure enough, he ends up on their lap.

Decreased social interaction and attempts to hide are indicators of emotional distress in a cat.

Felix

Felix belonged to an elderly lady who passed away. Her grandkids couldn't take him into their home so they gave him to the ARL. While working at ARL South, I felt so bad for him. He was extremely skinny and frightened, and he cried all the time. Felix also had the most unusual silver fur with reddish tabby markings. He was too unique and sad not to take home. He is my baby now and I've fattened him up to a normal weight. He greets me at the door and always tries to "help" with whatever I am doing whether it is laundry or cooking. While my other cat doesn't appreciate him, Felix and my dog love to wrestle and chase each other. Felix also loves to try to share my food, usually sticking his head right into my plate or cereal bowl. He went from the shelter to being a king and living in the lap of luxury. He is an integral part of my life now and I don't know what I would do without him.

Blaine and Alyssa

Mitch

A co-worker was considering adopting a cat and asked me to go to the ARL with her. I already had two cats so I thought I was safe accompanying her. We met a sweet one-and-a-half-year-old male with a little stump of a tail. We were told he had come in as a stray. We spent time cuddling and playing with him. The next day my co-worker decided now wasn't a good time to adopt a cat.

I was in trouble. All I could think about was that sweet cat with the little tail stump that would wiggle around. After spending only a short time with this cat, I was attached to him. That day I became an official rescue mom and Mitch (my new cat) got two new brothers.

For the first couple of days, Mitch spent his time in my study. I would let him out when I was home so he could get used to his new brothers. There was some establishment of the pecking order, but they all adapted fairly quickly.

Mitch and I, on the other hand, had a bit more of a challenge. I could tell he had been abused. He wouldn't let me walk up to him and if I tried to reach down and pet him, he would cringe. I talked to him a lot, so he would get used to my voice. I also found that if I sat on the floor and held my hand out, he would come up to me.

After a few months, Mitch started sleeping with me and even coming up and sitting on my lap. He would meet me at the door when I came home, then flop on the floor and want me to pet his belly.

After having him for a year and a half, I can't imagine our family without him. Even on my worst day, he always has the power to cheer me up. I'm thrilled to have provided a forever home for a deserving kitty, and I would recommend anyone else to do the same.

Crystal

- 🐾 spay/neuter

- 🐾 educate

- 🐾 adopt

- 🐾 volunteer

- 🐾 be active

- 🐾 donate

- 🐾 go home and hug your cat

What You Can Do to Help Cats

All of us who love our own cats also need to help other cats. Animal shelters across the country take in millions of cats, and they all need a second chance and a home.

The Animal Rescue League of Iowa (ARL) took in over 20,000 animals last year. Over half of those were cats and kittens. It is our responsibility to do what we can to help.

Spay/neuter

Spay or neuter your own cats and kittens, whether they go outside or not. One slip out the door for an unaltered cat can cause a pregnancy. If you hear a co-worker, friend or family member talking about his or her cats, ask if they are altered. If they aren't, help get them spayed or neutered, even if that means you have to pay to have it done. Make spaying and neutering a priority.

Educate

Educate your friends about the overpopulation problem. Make sure your friends know what is happening in the country with cat overpopulation. Get them engaged in helping to spread the word. Typically, people don't want to hear sad stories, but the overpopulation problem IS sad, and people need to hear it so we can work together to get the problem solved.

Adopt

If you are looking for a cat or kitten, adopt one from a shelter. There are wonderful cats of every age, breed, color, personality and gender in every animal shelter in this country. Save a life. Adopt. Even better - adopt two!

Some happy endings

from the Animal Rescue League of Iowa

Reprinted with permission, dsm Magazine

Snowball

Ever since I was a little girl, I have loved cats. Unfortunately, it was the one animal my parents would not allow me to have since I was extremely allergic. Even so, every Christmas I would ask for a cat.

When I was eight, I specifically asked for a white, fluffy cat with blue eyes named "Snowball." One Christmas morning, I got a *stuffed* white, fluffy cat with blue eyes; nonetheless, I named her Snowball.

After I graduated from high school and got my first apartment I was determined to adopt a cat, despite my allergies. Spanky, a Domestic Shorthair, gray kitten became my new roommate. As it turns out I had actually outgrown my allergy to cats so soon after I also adopted Capone, a Maine Coon.

Over the next several years, I adopted three large dogs, bringing the total of animals in my house to five. I decided I was at *my* limit for animals. One morning I walked into the ARL and saw a litter of kittens. There, among several other kittens, was a fluffy white cat with blue eyes. I cannot even tell you what the shelter had named her because from the moment I saw her, I thought, "It's Snowball!".

Already having my self-imposed "limit" of animals, I had absolutely zero intentions of adopting another animal, so when I saw she already had two adoption applications I was a little relieved. Throughout the rest of the day, I could not get her out of my head. It was eerie that exactly 20 years after getting my stuffed animal, Snowball, I saw the cat I had always envisioned. I couldn't fight fate, so the next day I decided I would apply to be third in line and if it worked out, it was meant to be and if not, she would still have a great home with someone else. Well, it was meant to be. The first applicant called and changed their mind and the second never showed up. Their deadline to adopt her was at noon, so at 12:01 p.m. I was completing the adoption contract to bring Snowball home.

Snowball taught me that you cannot always choose the pets you are destined to be with and despite "my limit", there was still room in my heart and my home for one more.

Snowball's story was 20 years in the making and now that she is one year old, I look forward to spending the next 20 years living *with* her instead of just dreaming *of* her.

Stephanie

Gone to a Good Home!

Volunteer

Take the extra time you have, whether it is one hour or one day a week and volunteer your time at a local animal shelter. Work at an event, clean cages, socialize cats, help with adoptions – just volunteer and make a difference. People say they can't volunteer because it makes them sad, but the cats need you. At least the cats and kittens at shelters, no matter what their fate, are in a safe place with food, shelter, and love versus out on the streets trying to survive.

Be Active

Be involved and active. Be active in animal protection legislation. If your community doesn't have mandatory spay/neuter laws, get involved in the legislative process and see what you can get done to get a spay/neuter law passed.

Donate

Donate money to your local animal shelter. They love the animals they care for, and it costs money to feed them and provide veterinary care. Donate whatever you can; it all makes a difference.

Go Home and Hug Your Cat

At the end of the workday, go home and hug your cat. Make a commitment to your cat that he will always be cared for. Make arrangements with a trusted family member or friend so if something happens to you, they will take your cat and care for him. Write the arrangements down and give multiple copies to family, a lawyer and a friend. Some states even allow pet trusts to be set up. If your state does, set one up to care for your cat.

Get Involved

For twenty years I have spent time in animal shelter work. I have seen things I wish I had not, and heard things I wish I had not. But at the same time, those things have changed and had a profound effect on me. Every day is a challenge at an animal shelter, but I have always gotten more than I have given in one way or another. Get involved and help. The cats are counting on you.

Make a commitment to your cat that you will care for him, or arrange care for him, for his *lifetime*.

Sophie & Titus

I adopted Titus and Sophie (Shelby) from the ARL (Main) on February 25, 2010. My cat of 15 years died in January 2010 and it was such a hard loss that I had decided I didn't want any more. My niece eventually talked me in to going to the ARL just to look and after several trips we saw this cute little kitten but he was hardly ever in his cage. When one of the volunteers came and asked us if we needed help we told her we wanted to see him but he must be popular because he kept disappearing. She told us that was because when you stood near his cage on the inside he played with your hair and when you didn't he cried until you came and got him. We fell in love with him but were 5 minutes late for the adoption process. This turned out to be a blessing because I got on the ARL website that night knowing that I would eventually get two so he would have a play mate and that's when I found Miss Sophie. We met her the next day and the volunteer that helped us told us what a sweetheart she was. Both of them had been found outside and the volunteers weren't sure if they had been around other cats. There was some concern that Sophie being the 1 year old shy cat might not be too sure about this ornery little 4 month old boy but we decided to give it a try. We brought them home that night and once they had thoroughly checked out their new digs they started to play together and have been best buddies ever since. They are so good together and I've never heard either of them hiss at the other. When they lay together it's rare that you don't see one or the other with their paw stretched out touching the other one. Titus is still the ornery little boy we met that night. If there is food anywhere around him unattended watch out. I remember one of our first days together I put two pieces of toast in the toaster and left for a moment and came back to find only one piece left. Sure enough Titus had taken the other piece. When we come in from outside and I take off his harness he cries at the back door and then puts his paws on the handle to try to open it. He is just like a curious little boy and watches everything you do. Sophie is the little sweetheart we were told she was. I discovered early on that she likes to give nose kisses. I saw her on several occasions touch noses with Titus so I made a kissing sound and she came right over and touched her nose to mine. She curls up next to me on the couch at night and gently works my hand around until she can get my thumb in her mouth to suck on it. I have never had any animals quite like these two. They are both so sweet and loving and full of personality. They put a smile on my face daily and I'm so grateful that my niece talked me in to going to the ARL after my loss because I can't imagine life without them!

Laurie

Gone to a
Good Home!

A Thank You from the Publisher

Landauer wishes to acknowledge and thank the many people who tirelessly and with great compassion care for the animals surrendered to shelters and especially those who worked to make this book happen. Their fondest wish is that there would be no need for animal shelters. Yet, shelters are and will always be needed. Each of us can help—whether adopting, volunteering at, or financially supporting our shelters.

We can spay and neuter.

We can train good behaviors.

We can report abuse.

The animals need each of us.

In particular, Landauer wishes to thank Carol Griglione, president of the board of directors of the Animal Rescue League of Iowa, who drawing on her more than 15 years experience specifically focused on cats, cat issues and behaviors has spent countless hours developing ARL of Iowa's book *For Love of Cats* and making sure the advice and guidance given here is what cat owners most need to know to live successfully with their cats. Thank you Carol!

And, thank you also to Mick McAuliffe. In addition to managing ARL – Iowa shelter operations, and training and counseling pet owners on pet behavior issues, Mick has been there whenever needed to assist in preparing and reviewing *For Love of Cats*.

Landauer also wishes to thank the following people who readily gave time and effort:

- Dr. Dan Campbell, Chief Staff Veterinarian, ARL-Iowa Main Shelter

- Stephanie Filer, Manager Special Gifts & Partnerships, ARL-Iowa

- Owners whose cats you see and read about in the rescue stories and photos

- Carol McGarvey, Contributing Editor

- And to the entire ARL-Iowa staff

- Special thanks to Tom Colvin, Executive Director, ARL-Iowa whose vision and dedication along with Carol's, has created the state-of-the-art animal shelter that is Animal Rescue League of Iowa.

- Finally, a thank you to the Landauer Staff whose standards-of-excellence and teamwork are second to none.

....

Resources:

Animal Rescue League of Iowa; www.arl-iowa.org

Humane Society of the United States; www.humanesociety.org

The American Society for the Prevention of Cruelty to Animals (ASPCA); www.aspca.org

American Humane Association; www.americanhumane.org

Animal Veterinary Medical Association; www.avma.org

Alley Cat Allies, Trap-Neuter-Return Program for feral cats; www.alleycat.org

Dr. Kersti Seksel, Registered Veterinary Specialist, Behavioral Medicine; www.sabs.com.au

Dr. Gaille Perry, Veterinary Behaviorist; www.sabs.com.au

Dr. Amy Marder, Director of the Center for Shelter Dogs; www.arlboston.org

Dr. Amanda Gigler; www.ankenyvets.com

12/13

For Love of **CATS**

SUPPORT YOUR LOCAL SHELTER